The American Economy, 1929-1970

The American Economy 1929-1970

Resources, Production, Income Distribution, and Use of Product, An Introduction

by Karl W. Roskamp
WAYNE STATE UNIVERSITY

WAYNE STATE UNIVERSITY PRESS
DETROIT, 1977

Title of original edition: Die Amerikanische Wirtschaft, 1929–1970. *Stuttgart: Alfred Kröner Verlag,* © *1975.*

Library of Congress Cataloging in Publication Data

Roskamp, Karl W
   The American economy, 1929–1970.

   Translation of Die amerikanische Wirtschaft.
   Bibliography: p. 170
   Includes index.
     1. United States—Economic conditions—1918–1945.
   2. United States—Economic conditions—1945–
   I. Title.
   HC106.6.R813   330.9′73′09   76-27318
   ISBN 0-8143-1554-2

Contents

Maps and Illustrations

Tables

Preface

The present volume is the English version of an introductory book on the American economy the author was asked to write for German-speaking readers.* The book is intended for beginning students in economics and other persons interested in the characteristics and problems of the American economy.

The task was to present to these readers, within a small book, in a concise but nontechnical manner, essential features of the economy. To do this it was decided to discuss in nine short chapters the nation's productive resources, its production, the income and property distribution, and the use of the national product. The last chapter states the main problems of the contemporary American economy. From the wealth of data on the economy, those were selected and presented in forty-two tables which seemed to be most useful in giving the student an idea of the magnitudes involved and in helping him understand important relationships discussed in the text. In all cases the data sources are given fully to facilitate further, independent study. The hope is that this volume may benefit English speaking students who try to understand the complex and rapidly changing American economy.

In retrospect, the years after 1972 proved to be more

*The German edition appeared under the title *Die Amerikanische Wirtschaft* (Stuttgart: Kröner Verlag, 1975).

difficult for the economy than was expected. This was partly because of international events which could not be foreseen. Yet, it is our belief that a look at the development of the economy between 1929 and 1970 helps to put the latest, not so favorable, events into proper perspective. As far as the main problems of the economy are concerned, we think that they are correctly stated. In 1975 they still existed and were more urgent than in any other post-World War II year.

It is a pleasure to acknowledge the help of several persons in the preparation of the manuscript for this book. I should like to thank Professor Romney Robinson of St. Légier, Switzerland, Professor Wolfgang F. Stolper of the University of Michigan, and Professor Horst C. Recktenwald of the Universität Erlangen-Nürnberg, West Germany, who initiated and encouraged the writing of this book, for a careful reading of the whole manuscript and the many helpful comments they made. In addition I should like to thank Professors Harold J. Barnett of Washington University in St. Louis, Lloyd G. Reynolds of Yale University, and Richard S. Eckaus of the Massachusetts Institute of Technology for helpful suggestions.

My thanks are further due to the United States Bureau of Census for the kind permission to reproduce for this volume some diagrams from the *Statistical Abstract of the United States.* Finally, it is my special pleasure to thank Miss Carol Temple of the Department of Economics at Wayne State University, Detroit, Michigan, for the diligent and skillful typing and retyping of the manuscript.

1.
Population

Growth of Population

The United States of America, surpassed in size only by the
U.S.S.R., Canada, and the People's Republic of China, has a
gifted and industrious population of sundry ethnological ori-
gins, adhering to different religions, cultural patterns, and
political views. According to the census of 1970, the population of the United States amounted to 203.2 million people. If
present population trends continue, the number may exceed
235 million in 1985.

The population of the United States has rapidly increased. The first census, in August 1790, counted within the
area of what was then the United States a population of 3.9
million people. Within a span of 180 years there was thus a
population growth of 199.3 million. This growth was the result of a continual excess of births over deaths and a net
immigration to the United States. It is estimated that the total
number of immigrants to the United States amounted to 45.2
million between 1820 and 1970.

The population growth was not uniform. The largest
increases occurred between 1790 and 1860, when the country was predominantly rural; decennial increases were then

TABLE 1
Population and Area of the United States 1790 to 1970

		Total Area		Inhabitants per mi.² of land area	Inhabitants per km.² of land area
Year	Population (millions)	1000 mi.²	1000 km.²		
1790	3.93	889	2,302	4.5	1.7
1820	9.64	1,788	4,631	5.5	2.1
1850	23.19	2,993	7,752	7.9	3.1
1880	50.15	3,022	7,827	16.9	6.5
1910	91.97	3,022	7,827	31.0	12.0
1940	131.67	3,022	7,827	44.2	17.1
1950*	151.32	3.615	9,363	42.6	16.4
1960*	179.32	3,615	9,363	50.5	19.5
1970*	203.18	3,615	9,363	57.4	22.2

Source: U.S. Bureau of Census, Statistical Abstract of the United States: 1971 (Washington, D.C., 1971), p. 5, table 1.
*including Alaska and Hawaii

between 32.7% and 36.4%. They diminished after 1860. The lowest increase (7.2%) was registered for the Great Depression decade, 1930–40 (see table 1). Subsequent decades showed higher growth rates. Between 1940 and 1950 the increase was 14.5%, and between 1950 and 1960 it even reached 18.5%. In the 1960–70 decade, the rate of increase fell off somewhat, to 13.3%.

Between April 1, 1960 and December 31, 1970, the population growth was 24.3 million. During this period the white population increased by 12% and that of all other races by 25%.[1] For the white population the increase through births was 20.4%, the decrease through deaths 10.1%, and the increase due to net immigration 1.7%. For all other races, the increase through births was 31.9%. Their death rate was somewhat higher than for the white population, namely 10.8%. The increase through net immigration was 3.9% for other races.

The population growth in the earlier period of the nation's history reflects the country's territorial expansion. Each decade the population center of the country moved further

CENTER OF POPULATION, 1790 TO 1970.

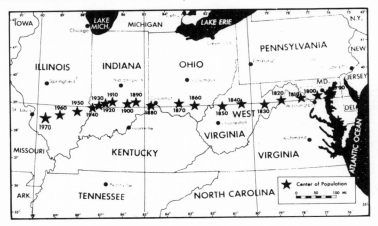

Fig. 1. Reproduced from U.S. Bureau of Census, *Statistical Abstract of the United States: 1972*, p. 6.

westward.[2] In 1790, when the population lived essentially along the Atlantic shore, the center was located 23 miles east of Baltimore, Maryland. By 1970 it was found about 50 miles southeast of St. Louis, Missouri, some 680 miles (1,100 km.) further west.

A higher population growth rate in the western states than in the northern and eastern states caused this continuous westward shift in the population center. Though the overall population increase between 1960 and 1970 was 13.3%, there was considerable regional variation. Comparing U.S. Bureau of Census regions, growth for the Northeast region amounted to 12.7%. For the Middle Atlantic region, which includes the populous state of New York, it was 8.7%. The West North Central region had a growth of only 6%. By comparison, the Pacific region, which includes California, experienced an increase in population of 25.1%. For the Mountain region the increase was 20.8%. In the eastern half of the country, only the South Atlantic region had a larger than average population increase, showing a growth of 18.1% between 1960 and 1970.[3] This growth in the southern regions of

MAP OF THE UNITED STATES, SHOWING CENSUS REGIONS AND DIVISIONS.

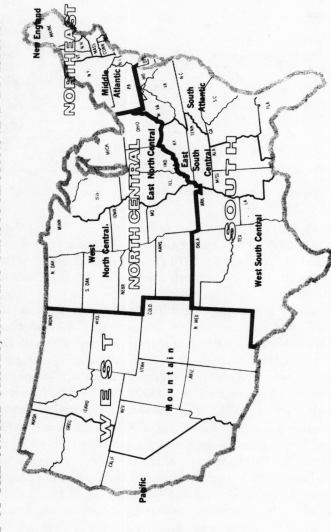

Fig. 2. Reproduced from U.S. Bureau of Census, *Statistical Abstract 1972*, p. xii. (Not shown are Alaska and Hawaii, which belong to the Pacific region, which is part of the larger West region.)

TABLE 2
Population Increases by Regions, 1960–70

Region	% Change
More than average for United States:	
South Atlantic	18.1
West South Central	14.0
Mountain	20.8
Pacific	25.1
Less than average for United States:	
North East	12.7
Middle Atlantic	8.7
East North Central	11.1
West North Central	6.0
East South Central	6.3

Source: Statistical Abstract 1971, p. 11, table 10.
Note: The regions are indicated on fig. 2.

the country shifted the population center not only west but also south. It has moved southwest since 1910.

The net migration between different regions of the United States is summarized in table 3. Though it is difficult to assess the magnitude of net migration statistically, the available data nevertheless reveal some important trends. The white population (including immigrants from abroad) has tended to move predominantly to the Pacific and the South Atlantic regions from the Middle Atlantic and the East and West North Central regions. In these regions the departing white population was partly replaced by Negroes migrating from southern regions. The gradient of white migration is from north and northeast to west and southeast, whereas the gradient of the Negro migration is essentially south to north.

The future population growth of the United States is a much discussed problem. Concern has grown about a deterioration of environmental factors vital for a healthy and happy life such as clean air and water, unspoiled forests,

TABLE 3

Net Migration of White and Negro Population between Regions of the United States 1960–70 (1,000 persons)

Region	White Population	Negro Population	Total White and Negro Population
New England	+ 205	+ 72	+ 277
Middle Atlantic	− 724	+ 540	− 184
East North Central	− 617	+ 356	− 261
West North Central	− 655	+ 26	− 629
South Atlantic	+1,807	− 538	+1,269
East South Central	− 153	− 560	− 713
West South Central	+ 152	− 282	− 130
Mountain	+ 295	+ 16	+ 311
Pacific	+1,974	+ 286	+2,260

Source: Statistical Abstract 1971, p. 15.

Note: Total resident population. Comprises net immigration from abroad and net migration between regions. Includes movement of persons of Armed Forces.

recreational land, and quiet uncongested places. A too-rapid population growth could endanger the environment. Crowding could indeed precipitate great sociological and economic problems. There has been in the United States some discussion about the advisability of a much lower rate of population growth. Some have even advocated a zero growth rate. Among social scientists there is as yet no consensus as to what is an "optimal population" or, for that matter, an "optimal population growth."

Estimates of the future population growth of the United States are based on past demographic developments. This growth depends on a host of interrelated sociological, psychological, economic, and medical factors. Extrapolations, however refined and adjusted, must be considered with some caution. In view of the difficulties in predicting population growth, economists have usually preferred to take it as a given exogenous factor in economic analysis. Yet it is desirable to have at least a rough idea about the magnitudes of possible future population increases.

TABLE 4
*Projected Population for the United States
in 1975, 1980, 1985, and 1990
(In Millions of Persons)*

Assumption	1975	1980	1985	1990
1	219.1	236.8	257.0	277.3
2	217.6	232.4	249.2	266.3
3	215.6	227.5	240.9	254.7
4	214.7	225.5	236.9	247.7

Source: Statistical Abstract 1971, p. 8, table 6. Figures are rounded off.

The official *Statistical Abstract 1971* provides four projections based on census data.[4] For all of them it is assumed that the future net immigration to the United States will be 400,000 persons annually. Since the most critical parameter is then the birthrate, different assumptions have been made about it in each projection. For the first, it is assumed that in future years the average number of children per 1,000 women at the end of the childbearing age will be 3,100. The second projection assumes that the number of children will be 2,775. The third assumption is 2,450 children and the fourth, 2,100. Table 4 shows the projected population under each of the four assumptions.

Characteristics of the Population

The population of the United States consists of a variety of races. For statistical purposes, only three large groups are usually distinguished: whites, Negroes, and "all others." "All others" is a rather heterogeneous group consisting essentially of American Indians, Japanese, Chinese, Filipinos, Asian Indians, Koreans, Polynesians, Indonesians, Hawaiians, Aleuts, and Eskimos.[5] In 1960, 88.6% of the population were white, 10.5% were Negro, and 0.9%, all other races.[6] In 1970 whites accounted for 87.4% of the total population, Negroes for 11.2%, and all other races for 1.4%.

Until 1940 the male population in the United States was always somewhat larger than the female one. Today the country has more females than males. In 1970 there were about 105 females for 100 males.[7]

There have also been changes in the age distribution of the total population. In 1960, 31.1% of the population was less than 15 years old. In 1970 only 28.5% belonged to this age group, a reflection of the lower birth rate in the decade 1960–70. The age bracket of from 15 to 24 years was, on the other hand, a numerous one in 1970, containing 17.4% of the population, compared to 13.4% in 1960. The members of this age bracket were born during the so-called baby boom in the years following World War II. The 25-to-44-year bracket accounted in 1960 for 26.1% of the population; in 1970 for 23.7%. People over 44 years old made up 29.3% of the total in 1960 and 30.4% in 1970. These structural changes are important, for they affect the social security system, the demand for educational facilities, and other population-related public goods. Yet one cannot readily infer from them "the age" of the population. Indeed, according to the median age, the population was in 1970 a little "younger" than in 1960. In 1960 the median was 29.5 years (30.3 years for whites and 23.5 for Negroes), and in 1970 it was 28.3 years (29.1 for the white and all other races and 22.8 for Negroes).[8]

Because the economic decisions of an individual are usually influenced by the needs and the welfare of the household in which he lives, it is useful to consider the household structure of the American population. In most cases "the household" means a husband-wife family; but a person living alone, or a group of unrelated persons sharing the same housing unit as partners, is also counted as a household in the United States. Keeping this definition in mind, we may consider a few historical figures. In 1890 the number of households in the United States was 12.69 million. The average number of people per household was at that time 4.93. Since then in each decade the number of households has increased. In March 1970 they totalled 62.87 million. Yet between 1890

and 1970 the average number of people per household decreased, dropping to 3.17 persons in 1970. The Department
of Commerce estimates that in 1985 there will be between
81.2 and 84.4 million households, depending on marriage
and household status assumptions.[9] The average number of
people per household is likely to be lower than in 1970.

Of the 62.9 million households in 1970, 51.2 million
were families. Of these, 44.4 million were husband-wife
families, 1.2 million families had a male head other than the
husband, and 5.5 million families had a female head. The
other households consisted of single individuals or non-
related individuals living together.[10] In the white population,
72.5% of all households were husband-wife households, 7.8%
had another male head, and 19.7% were headed by a female
member.[11] For the Negroes and all other races, only 54.7% of
all households were husband-wife households, 12.3% were
headed by another male head, and 33.0% were headed by a
female member.

The movement of the population from rural into urban
areas evidently influenced the household structure. For
farmers, husband-wife households still accounted for 81.6%
of all households in 1970. Only 9.3% of all farm households
had a female head.[12]

The United States was at the time of its foundation a
rural country; in 1790 only 5.4% of its population lived in
urban areas. Not until between 1910 and 1920 did more
people begin to live in urban areas than in rural ones. Since
then urbanization has markedly increased. The estimate is
that 73.5% of the population lived in urban areas in 1970—a
percentage which, by some predictions, will increase in the
decades to come. One expects that there will be in some
parts of the country extended urban agglomerations stretch-
ing over many miles, embedding in them present-day central
cities and urban areas.[13]

The distinction between urban and rural areas is, however, too general because it veils important shifts in the residence of the American population. What an urban area is

POPULATION CHANGES IN METROPOLITAN AREAS, BY RACE, 1950–60 AND 1960–70.

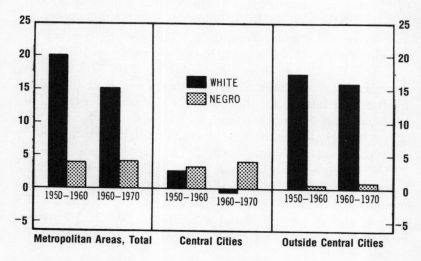

Fig. 3. Reproduced from U.S. Bureau of Census, *Statistical Abstract 1972*, p. 4.

exactly is difficult to say; its definition must be left to specialists in that field. Today most American urban areas have two distinct parts, the "central cities" and the "suburban areas." The latter are sometimes again subdivided into "urban fringe" and "outside urbanized areas."

During the past two decades the white population has tended to leave the central cities (also called core cities or inner cities) and to move towards the suburban areas. The Negro population, on the other hand, has moved into the central cities, leaving rural areas. Table 5 indicates these major movements.

During the decade 1960–70 the white population, despite its rapid growth, actually *decreased* in the central cities. The number of white inhabitants of central cities was 49.44 million in 1960 but decreased to 48.80 million in 1970.[14] On the other hand, in 1970 there were 15.9 million more whites in the urban areas (outside central cities) than in 1960. The

TABLE 5
Population by Residence and Race,
1950–70
(Percentage Distribution)

	1950	1960	1970
White Population			
Central Cities	34.6	31.1	27.5
Outside Central Cities	28.3	35.1	40.3
Nonmetropolitan Areas	37.0	33.8	32.2
Total	100.0	100.0	100.0
Negro Population			
Central Cities	44.3	52.7	57.8
Outside Central Cities	14.8	14.9	16.3
Nonmetropolitan Areas	40.9	32.4	26.0
Total	100.0	100.0	100.0

Source: Statistical Abstract 1971, p. 16, table 14.

white population in nonmetropolitan areas also *increased* by 3.5 million.

The Negro population in the central cities *increased* during 1960–70 by 3.14 million. Its increase in urban areas (outside central cities) was a mere 0.9 million. The Negro population in nonmetropolitan areas *decreased* by 0.2 million.

These population shifts are caused by a variety of sociological, psychological, and economic factors. They are of major importance for the American nation and have far-reaching implications for its private and public economy.

Education

Human beings are not born with wisdom and knowledge. Each generation must learn, de novo, in a long and costly educational process, what preceding generations knew in order to maintain—and to add to—the store of existing knowledge.

Education has a value that is in general larger than the direct economic benefits its recipient can derive from it. A well-educated person is likely to be a more civilized and cultured citizen. Education may make him a more valuable member of the society in which he lives. These are important intangible values deriving from a good education. In the context of this book we are mainly interested, however, in the economic implication of education which is, admittedly, only one of its many aspects.

Sophisticated and complex economies need an educated population. It has been argued that each human being is, in his ability to perform productive work, endowed with two factors of production. The first is "raw labor," which permits him to perform simple physical work. The second is "human capital," which enables him to perform tasks requiring knowledge and skills. Whereas raw labor may be considered as inborn and given, human capital must be formed. The formation depends to a large extent on the education and training a person receives.

Formal education at all levels in the United States is provided by two different types of schools, public and private. In 1968 there were 70.9 thousand public and 14.9 thousand private elementary schools.[15] For secondary education there were 27.0 thousand public and 4.4 thousand private schools. Higher education was provided by 934 public and 1,440 private colleges and universities. During the last forty years the number of schools for both secondary and higher education increased. The number of elementary schools diminished as more and more small, one-teacher schools were replaced by larger, multiple-teacher schools. The total enrollment in all schools was estimated at 59.2 million students in 1970. Of these, 37.1 million were at the elementary level, 14.7 million in secondary schools, and 7.4 million at institutions of higher education.[16]

Tax-supported public institutions now provide the primary and secondary education for most American children. At the elementary level, 88.4% of all students were enrolled in public schools and 11.6% in private ones in 1970.[17] In the same year 92% of all high school students attended public schools and only 8% went to private ones. At the college and university level, 77% of all students enrolled in public institutions and 23% in private ones. Because of family tradition, or the desire for social prestige or better quality instruction, some parents send their offspring to private schools, which are supported mainly by fees for each attending student. The emphasis on private education is more marked at the "higher," college or university, level. Though there were 1,440 private higher education institutions in 1970, compared to 934 public ones, a public college or university ordinarily enrolls many more students than a private one. The typical public higher education institution was a state university with from 10,000 to 25,000 or more students; the typical private institution would have from 1,500 to 5,000 students.

Between 1950 and 1970, U.S. school enrollments increased dramatically at all levels. Elementary school enrollment rose by about 73%. For high schools it more than doubled; in colleges and universities, it more than tripled. The increase in enrollment of women in colleges and universities during this period was especially spectacular. In 1970, more than 3 million women were enrolled, more than four times the number enrolled in 1950.

Not only were there more students; those who studied completed more years at school. Table 6, which shows the number of school years completed for persons of age 25 years and over for selected years from 1940 on, clearly reveals the tendency to stay longer in school and to receive a more advanced education. By 1970 the Negro population had also made considerable advances in this direction, though it still lagged substantially behind the rest of the population.

Much of the demand for higher education is no doubt economically motivated. It is no secret that a better educa-

TABLE 6
Years of School Completed, by Race,
1940–70

	All Persons of Age 25 years and over (%)			
	1940	1950	1960	1970
All Races				
Less than 5 years of elementary school	13.7	11.1	8.3	5.3
High School, 4 years or more	24.5	34.3	41.1	55.2
College, 4 years or more	4.6	6.2	7.7	11.0
Median School years completed, in years	8.6	9.3	10.5	12.2
Negro Population				
Less than 5 years of elementary school	42.0	32.9	23.8	15.1
High School, 4 years or more	7.3	12.9	20.1	33.7
College, 4 years or more	1.3	2.1	3.1	4.5
Median School years completed, in years	5.7	6.8	8.0	9.9

Source: Statistical Abstract 1971, p. 109, table 164.
Population of age 25 years and over is 100%.

tion opens access to better-paid professions. The available
data indicate that the majority of employees with less than
four years of high school education were blue collar workers
or working in the lower paying occupations. It has been estimated that on the average a person with eight years of elementary school could, in 1967, expect a lifetime income of
$192,000. With a four-year high school education, the esti-
mated lifetime income was estimated at $257,000; and with a
college education of four years or more, it was $437,000.[18]
Today the main concern of many American families is to

assure for the children an education that will permit them to form enough human capital to be successful in a competitive world.

Literature

Spengler, Joseph J. "Population Theory." In *A Survey of Contemporary Economics*, vol. 2, edited by Bernard F. Haley. Homewood, Ill.: American Economic Association, Richard D. Irwin Co., 1952, and the many sources listed therein.
For U.S. government publications, up to 1957, see:
U.S. Department of Commerce. *Historical Statistics of the United States, Colonial Times to 1957*, chap. A, pp. 1–6. Washington, D.C., 1960.
For the latest data, see:
U.S. Department of Commerce, Bureau of Census. *United States Census of Population: 1970*, vol. 1. Washington, D.C.

2.
Labor Force

Economists have traditionally distinguished three factors of production, labor, capital, and land. Labor was provided by the working population, capital consisted of reproducible capital goods, and land was given by nature. Nowadays only two factors of production are usually considered in the analysis of the productive process in advanced industrial nations, labor and reproducible capital. The factor land is considered of subordinate importance in this process.[1]

Production theories try to explain in what ways labor and capital combine, given a certain state of technology, to produce the goods and services the population desires. By necessity, production theories have to simplify as to the nature of the productive factors. In production functions, labor and capital are often treated as large, homogenous aggregates.[2] In reality, both are heterogeneous. Each has a structure. The labor force of a country has a certain age composition and a regional distribution; its members have widely differing qualifications, and they are employed in a variety of economic sectors. Part of the labor force may be organized in trade unions.

A Total Picture of the Labor Force

The U.S. Bureau of Census defines "labor force" as the sum of the country's employed and unemployed adults.* In 1940, the U.S. labor force consisted of 56.2 million persons. By 1970, the number had risen to 85.9 million, an increase of 29.7 million in thirty years.

As of April 1971, the labor force comprised 85.8 million persons. Of these, 82.9 million belonged to the civilian labor force and 2.9 million to the armed forces. Department of Labor data show that 59.6% of the population 16 years and older were in the civilian labor force. The percentage is called the labor force participation rate. It rose slightly during the last decade, from 58.1% in 1960 to 59.0% in 1970.[3]

Of the 82.9 million persons in the civilian labor force, 78.2 million were employed, 3.5 million in agriculture and 74.7 million in all other sectors of the economy. Unfortunately, the country has always had some unemployment. Though unemployment after World War II was not as high as in the prewar years, it did reach 4.8 million in 1961. In February 1971, 4.7 million persons were unemployed. Figures for other years are shown in table 7.

Of the population of age 16 and older, 56.3 million persons were not in the labor force in April 1971. Housewives and other persons keeping house accounted for 35.4 million of these and persons attending school for another 9.2 million.

---

*According to the *Statistical Abstract 1971* (p. 218), employed persons comprise all those over 14 (since January 1967 all persons over 16) "who, during the survey week of each month, did any work for pay or profit, worked 15 hours or more as unpaid workers in family enterprises, or did not work but had jobs or businesses from which they were temporarily absent for noneconomic reasons." "Unemployed persons comprise all persons not working during the survey week who had made specific efforts to find a job within the past four weeks and who were available for work, and persons who were on layoff from a job or waiting to report to a new wage or salary job within 30 days." See also *Concepts and Methods Used in Manpower Statistics from the Current Population Survey,* report no. 313, Bureau of Labor Statistics, Department of Labor, Washington, D.C.

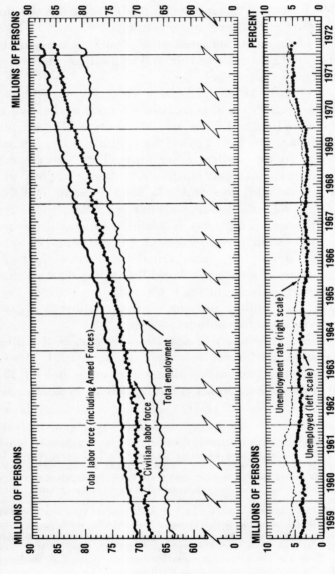

Fig. 4. Chart prepared by U.S. Bureau of Census. Data for January-June 1959 from U.S. Bureau of Census; thereafter, from U.S. Bureau of Labor Statistics. Reproduced from *Statistical Abstract 1972*, p. 212.

TABLE 7
Labor Force of the United States,
1940–70
(Millions of Persons)

Year	Total, including Armed Forces	Civilian Labor Force Total	Unemployed	Unemployed as % of Civ.LaborForce
1940	56.2	55.6	8.1	14.6
1945	65.3	53.9	1.0	1.9
1950	64.7	63.1	3.3	5.3
1955	68.9	65.8	2.9	4.4
1960	73.1	70.6	3.9	5.6
1961	74.2	71.6	4.8	6.7
1962	74.7	71.8	4.0	5.6
1963	75.7	73.0	4.2	5.7
1964	75.8	73.1	3.8	5.2
1965	77.2	74.4	3.4	4.5
1966	78.9	75.8	2.9	3.8
1967	80.8	77.3	3.0	3.8
1968	82.3	78.7	2.8	3.6
1969	84.2	80.7	2.8	3.5
1970	85.9	82.7	4.1	4.9
1971, Apr.	85.8	82.9	4.7	5.7

Sources: For 1940 to 1963, *Statistical Abstract 1967*, p. 218, table 308; for 1964 to 1970, *Statistical Abstract 1971*, p. 210, table 327.

Note: Years prior to 1960 exclude Alaska and Hawaii. All figures are rounded off.

It should be observed that the division between persons "in the labor force" and persons "not in the labor force" cannot be concise. Some persons (especially housewives) who are generally not in the labor force may decide to work temporarily if there are attractive employment possibilities or if it is necessary to increase the family income. In case of a national emergency many persons normally not in the labor force could no doubt enter it. In 1940, just before the country entered World War II, there were 44.2 million persons not in the labor force; by 1945, the last war year, there were 40.2 million. During the war, the number of unemployed fell from 8.1 million (1940) to one million (1945).[4]

TABLE 8
The Age Structure of the Labor Force, 1970

Age Bracket	Male Labor Force		Female Labor Force	
Years	Persons in Mill.	%	Persons in Mill.	%
16–17	1.84	3.4	1.32	4.2
18–19	2.56	4.7	1.93	6.1
20–24	7.38	13.6	4.89	15.5
25–34	11.97	22.0	5.70	18.1
35–44	10.82	19.9	5.97	18.9
45–54	10.49	19.3	6.53	20.7
55–64	7.13	13.1	4.15	13.2
65 and over	2.16	4.0	1.06	3.4
Total	54.35	100.0	31.55	100.0

Source: Statistical Abstract 1971, p. 211, table 328.
Note: Total labor force, including armed forces and unemployed.

Temporary entrance into the labor force may distort employment figures. Persons normally not in the labor force may decide to work, increasing the labor force. If they are entitled to unemployment benefits when their employment ceases, they may swell the list of the unemployed.

Characteristics of the Labor Force

The number of women relative to that of men in the American labor force has markedly increased during the last three decades. In 1940 the total labor force (including the Armed Forces and unemployed) consisted of 56.2 million persons. Of these, 42.0 million (74.7%) were men and 14.2 million (25.3%) women.[5] By 1960, the proportion of women in the total labor force had risen to 32%; by 1970 it was 37%. This may be the upper level; for 1985, the female share in the labor force is expected to remain at about 37%.

For each age bracket the participation rate in the labor force[6] was higher for men than for women (see table 9). In

TABLE 9
Labor Force Participation Rates,
1970

Age	Male Labor Force	Female Labor Force
16–17	46.7	34.6
18–19	68.8	53.4
20–24	85.1	57.5
25–34	95.0	44.8
35–44	95.7	50.9
45–54	92.9	54.0
55–64	81.5	42.5
65 and over	25.8	9.2

Source: Statistical Abstract 1971, p. 211, table 328.
Note: Total male or female population in each bracket is 100%.

1970, this ratio for men was 46.7% for the 16-to-17 year age bracket; it rose to 95.7% for ages 35–44 and fell to 25.8% after the retirement age of 65. For men, the participation rate thus had a single peak. The participation rate for women is somewhat different, reflecting the fact their employment is usually interrupted when they raise their families. Married life and young children often obligate them to stay temporarily at home. The 1970 participation ratio for women was 34.6% for the 16-to-17-year age group. It rose to 57.5% for the 20–24 bracket but fell to 44.8% for the 25–34 bracket. Once their children are somewhat older, many women begin to work again. For the 35–44 age group, therefore, the participation rate bounced back up to 50.9%; and it reached a second peak with 54% for the 45–54 age bracket. After that it fell. Only 9.2% of all women over 65 were still in the labor force in 1970. For biological reasons, the female participation ratio is double peaked.

The contribution women make to the work effort in the United States is impressive. In addition to 31.5 million women listed as being in the labor force in 1971, there were 35.1 million women "keeping house." Assuming that keeping house requires on the average at least as much effort as a professional activity, there were 66.6 million women contributing through their work effort to the welfare of the nation. This compares with 54.5 million men in the same year (54.2 million in the labor force and 0.3 million "keeping house").

In April 1971, about 10% of the male and 12.6% of the female civilian labor force were Negroes and members of other nonwhite races. There were 5.5 million male and 4.0 million female nonwhites in the civilian labor force.[7] The labor force participation rate for nonwhite men was lower and that of nonwhite women higher than for white men and women. The unemployment rate for nonwhites was generally higher than for whites. In 1961 unemployment for male nonwhites reached 12.9%; for female nonwhites 11.9%.[8] In April 1971 it was 8.1% for males and 10.8% for females. The corresponding April 1971 figures for the total labor force (including nonwhites) were 5.1% and 6.5%.

The American labor force is nowadays heavily concentrated in "urban agglomerations." Such agglomerations are now customarily defined in terms of a statistical unit called the "Standard Metropolitan Statistical Area" (SMSA).[9] For statistical analysis, all of the United States areas are distinguished as being "inside SMSAs" or "outside SMSAs." In general, a region inside an SMSA is a county or a group of contiguous counties that have one central city or an agglomeration of cities of at least 50,000 inhabitants. Of the total civilian labor force in 1970 of 82.7 million persons, 54.4 million were concentrated in the SMSAs.[10] SMSAs with 250,000 or more inhabitants had 46.6 million members of the civilian labor force. Of the remaining 28.3 million persons working outside of metropolitan areas, 24.6 million were nonfarm labor and 3.7 million, farm labor. Most Americans now work in urban or urbanized areas within which one finds the so-called inner cities, and in these the so-called urban poverty neighborhoods. In 1970, 6.2 million members of the civilian labor force worked in these areas, which have been characterized by high rates of unemployment—6.3% for the white and 9.5% for the nonwhite labor force in 1970.

Part of the labor force is now organized in unions, whose history is nearly as long as that of the United States.[11] From small local craftsmen's unions formed in the last decade of the eighteenth century, the present unions have developed in a long process of organizing, reorganizing, legal battles, adverse and favorable government decisions, and adjustment to changing economic and social conditions. Some have more than one million members. Most U.S. unions are joined in a loose federation, the American Federation of Labor— Congress of Industrial Organization (AFL-CIO), which has considerable political strength as a spokesman for labor.

U.S. membership in national and international unions amounted to 18.9 million in 1968. This number represents 23% of the total labor force and 27.9% of all employed labor in nonagricultural establishments.[12] Counting the 1.3 million Canadian members of American unions in 1968, the total membership was thus 20.2 million. It is to this figure that the following breakdowns refer.

Only a relatively small fraction of union members (15.7%) are white-collar workers; the majority are blue-collar workers. Male membership is much more important numerically (16.3 million) than that of females (3.9 million). About 15.6 million of all employees were affiliated with the AFL-CIO through their unions. Independent and nonaffiliated unions had 4.6 million members.

The degree of unionization in nonagricultural establishments varies by regions and states. In 1968 the lowest rate was 7.5% in North Carolina; the highest, 41.9% in West Virginia, a state dominated by coal mining. For many of the industrialized states unionization was between 30% and 37%.[13]

Trade union membership is very much concentrated in key industries, such as the automotive, trucking, iron and steel, and electrical equipment industries. Though union members account for not even a quarter of the total labor force, union influence in economic and social policy is much larger than this fraction might suggest. Unions have become, for good or bad, a permanent feature in the country's economic, social, and political life.

Literature

Bowen, William, and Finegan, T. A. *The Economics of Labor Force Participation.* Princeton, N.J.: Princeton University Press, 1969.

Cain, Glen G. *Married Women in the Labor Force: An Economic Analysis.* Chicago: University of Chicago Press, 1966.

Commons, John R., et al. *History of the Labor Movement in the United States.* 4 vols. New York: Macmillan Company, 1918.

Goldberg, Arthur J. *AFL-CIO Labor United.* New York: McGraw-Hill Company, 1956.

Long, Clarence D. *The Labor Force under Changing Income and Employment.* Princeton, N.J.: Princeton University Press, 1958.

Reynolds, Lloyd G. *Labor Economics and Labor Relations.* 5th ed. Englewood Cliffs, N.J.: Prentice-Hall, 1970.

3.
Natural Resources

We are concerned here only with those natural resources in which there is an economic interest. For our purposes, a natural resource is a substance found in nature that man knows how to recognize and utilize for satisfaction of his needs, a substance that can be used without any great transformation or change. Any necessary transformations or changes should be made without great cost in terms of other resources. Natural resources thus defined can be conveniently classified in six categories: soils of different types and qualities; wild growing plants of various kinds; wild animal life; water, which modern man uses in ever increasing quantities; minerals, which are extracted from the earth; and, finally, the atmosphere.

Land

According to data for 1970, the total land surface of the United States is 3.536 million square miles (9.191 million km.²) Of this, 46.5% was used for agriculture. This percentage is lower than for France (61.5) and West Germany (55.8),

TABLE 10

Land Use in the United States, 1964

USE	AREA		
	In 1000 mi.²	In 1000 km.²	%
Crop Land	681*	1,764*	18.8
Pasturage	1,000	2,591	27.7
Crop Land and Pasturage	1,681	4,356	46.5
Forests	1,143**	2,961**	31.6
Other Land	723	1,873	20.0
Total Land Area	3,549	9,191	98.2
Water Area	66	172	1.8
Total Area	3,615	9,363	100.0

Source: Statistisches Jahrbuch für die Bundesrepublik Deutschland 1971, p. 47, rounded values. Details may not add to total.
* For the year 1967.
** Without 46,332 mi.² (120,000 km.²) of reforested areas (Schonwälder).

TABLE 11

Total Land and Land for Agricultural Use in Other Countries

	Total Land		Agricultural Use		
	1000 km.²	1000 mi.²	1000 km.²	1000 mi.²	%
West Germany	243.33	93.95	135.78	52.42	55.8
France	547.03	211.21	336.29	129.80	61.5
Russia	22,402.00	8,649.00	5,980.00	2,309.00	26.7
China, People's Republic	9,561.00	3,691.00	2,873.00	1,109.00	30.0

Source: Statistisches Jahrbuch für die Bundesrepublik Deutschland 1971, p. 46.

but is considerably higher than for the Soviet Union (26.7) and the People's Republic of China (30.0). Forests account for 31.6% of American land. The rest is either unfit for agriculture and forests or used for buildings, roads, etc.

The United States is thus a large country with a high percentage of arable land. Its location in a zone of a generally favorable, moderate climate assures that it can be highly productive with appropriate human effort. Yet considerable regional differences in the quality of soil exist, ranging from the infertile Florida sands to some of the most fertile soils of the world in the country's corn belt.

Land in the United States was 58.6% privately owned in 1964. Indians held a small fraction (2.2%), and the rest (39.2%) was public land, most of it owned by the federal government (33.8%). The states owned 4.6% and counties and municipalities, 0.8%.[1] The largest part of land owned by the federal government is used for forests and serves among others as a habitat of wildlife. A large portion is used for grazing. The rest serves for such sundry purposes as military camps, airfields, and parks.

The value of the land of the United States is difficult to assess. According to some estimates, private farmland in the United States had in 1968 a value of $152.6 billion in current prices. Private nonfarm land was valued at $418.6 billion; land in the public domain at $144.2 billion.[2] Thus the total value of the tangible, nonreproducible asset, land, was estimated at $715.4 billion. Great as this value is, it constitutes only a fraction of total U.S. tangible assets (23.3%). The much larger share of the nation's assets is due to the efforts of man and is reproducible. To these we shall turn later.

Plant Life

The natural resource of wild plant life can be subdivided into three categories: natural vegetation in grasslands, the grasses and shrubs of the plains and deserts, and forests of different types. It is difficult to estimate the economic value of the first two resources in the United States. One of the best uses grasslands can be put to is grazing of livestock. A few figures may be given to indicate the extent of the use of this resource, assuming that it is still freely available without any great input of labor or capital and is thus a natural resource in the sense of the above definition. Of the federally owned land, 164,256,000 acres (664,735 km.²) were used for grazing. In the national forests, which are part of the federally owned land, grazed more than 1.6 million cattle, horses, and pigs and 2.2 million sheep and goats in 1969.³ The direct economic value of the forests of the United States is best reflected in the annual production of lumber, which amounted to 337.3 million cubic meters in 1968. This production is second only to that of the Soviet Union, which produced 380.4 million cubic meters in the same year.⁴

Natural resources stemming from plant life are not only important for their direct economic value. Such natural vegetation is also of great value because of its benevolent influence on the environment in which man lives. During recent years the American public has grown more aware of this aspect of plant-life natural resources. Various measures have been taken to prevent encroachments upon them.

Animal Life

Man makes use of the natural resource of animal life by hunting and fishing. Though hunting was economically important in the early stages of U.S. history it no longer is so. As more and more land was used for agriculture, the stock of game diminished in most regions. Today hunting is essentially a government-regulated sport in the United States. It is difficult to get information on the economic value of the hunted animals. More easily available are figures showing the number and cost of hunting licenses issued. In 1969, 21.6 million licenses were issued for a total price of $95.7 million.⁵

Inland and ocean fishing is, on the other hand, an important industry in the United States. It employed 217,000 people in 1968 and supplied 17.3 billion pounds (7.8 million metric tons) of fish.⁶ Fish and other sea creatures available from these waters are important for the nation's food supply and as industrial raw material.

Water

An abundant supply of good, fresh water is a resource of considerable value for a country's economy. Through the availability of appropriate equipment, it is nowadays possible to irrigate large areas and make them agriculturally useful. In addition to the traditional, direct use, sustaining life of men, animals, and plants, water has become industrially important as a supplier of energy in hydroelectric power plants and as an ingredient or coolant in many transformation processes. Besides this, water in navigable rivers, lakes, and canals is of economic value because it facilitates inland waterway transport and often permits establishment of recreational facilities on which tourist industries are based.

Available U.S. water resources vary widely by region, depending on topographical and meteorological conditions. In the humid eastern part of the country, water demands are generally met with little difficulty. Several large cities depend on the water of the Great Lakes, a uniquely large source of fresh water near the industrial heartland. Only in years of little rainfall have there been temporary shortages of water in large cities of the East and Midwest. For the arid lands of the West, however, water is often in short supply and must frequently be transported over great distances.

The city of Los Angeles, for instance, obtains water from the Colorado River, several hundred miles away. The Colorado symbolizes in a way the water needs of the American West. It was once a mighty river flowing into the Gulf of California. Today, numerous dams check its flow, and tunnels and aquaducts drain its water. The river produces large quantities of electricity, supplies millions of people with drinking water, and irrigates thousands of acres of land in the United States and Mexico. Nearly every drop of the river's water is somehow used. If any water finally reaches the ocean, it is only a little waste water from irrigation systems. In the years to come, the water demand of this region will increase. Thus a gigantic water supply project may become a reality. This project, the "North American Water and Power Alliance," envisages the channeling of large quantities of water from Alaska and western Canada to the United States and Mexico. The cost may be more than one hundred billion dollars. For the moment, however, this is only a plan for the future.

It is estimated that in 1900 the country used 40.2 billion gallons (152 million metric tons) of water. By 1940, this had risen to 136.4 billion gallons (516 million metric tons); and in 1970 it was 327.3 billion gallons (1,239 million metric tons). For 1980, the water use is estimated at 442.6 billion gallons (1,675 million metric tons).[7]

To assure such water availability, especially during dry seasons and years with less than normal rainfall, is a challenge, particularly since the water supply has a qualitative as well as quantitative dimension.[8] Some modern technological transformation processes require a large amount of water, which is often taken from rivers and lakes to be pumped back after it is used. If proper care is not taken, chemical or thermal pollution of water bodies may result, even if these are rather large. Lake St. Clair near Detroit was polluted by mercury in 1969–70, and shortly after that pollution in Lake Erie was so bad that the lake was considered "dead." Sewage disposal and spilling of oil create similar problems.

In 1970, U.S. water power generated about 265 billion kwh., or 16.2% of all electricity generated.[9] Though this was more than the total electricity production of West Germany or Great Britain, it represents only a fraction of the country's potential water power. There are still large unused water resources in the mountain and pacific regions.

Minerals

The United States is unusually well endowed with mineral resources, even though it must rely on imports for some its needs. It is impossible, however, to exactly outline the extent of these resources for the United States or any other country, for two reasons. First, the total of resources is always imprecisely known; new discoveries may change the picture drastically. Second, the physical presence of a mineral does not necessarily mean that it exists in sufficiently concentrated form, and sufficiently close to the earth's surface, to make its extraction economically feasible.[10] One can, however, summarize current estimates of mineral reserves, current domestic production, and current exports and imports. For this purpose, four essential categories must be distinguished: (1) coal mining, (2) oil and gas extraction, (3) metal mining, and (4) the mining of non-metallic minerals.

Coal Mining

The total coal reserves of the United States are believed to be 3,197 billion short tons (2,900 billion metric tons), half of which can probably be mined. This amount is vastly superior to that of Europe or the U.S.S.R. The U.S.S.R. reserves are believed to be 426 billion metric tons. The coal reserves of mainland China may be as large as 995 billion metric tons; considerable uncertainty seems to surround this figure.[11]

The total coal production in the United States was 517.8 million metric tons in 1969.[12] Of this, 460.1 million metric tons were consumed domestically (279.7 million tons by electric power utilities and 168.5 million by manufacturing and mining industries). Another 51.0 million tons were exported. Imports amounted to a mere 90,700 tons.

Oil and Gas Extraction

The "proved" reserves of crude petroleum as of 31 December 1970 were given as 39 billion barrels, each barrel containing 42 gallons.[13] Of these, 10.1 billion were in Alaska, 3.9 billion in California, 5.7 billion in Louisiana, and 13.2 billion in Texas. Domestic production amounted to 3.517 billion barrels in 1970.

During the last twenty years the country's share in world production has been decreasing. In 1950 it amounted to 52%, but it fell to 22% in 1969.[14] In the same period, imports of crude petroleum rose. In 1969 the country imported 514 million barrels of crude petroleum, whereas exports were negligible. In addition to crude petroleum, 641 million barrels of refined petroleum products were also imported. To satisfy the enormous consumption of gasoline and other petroleum fuels, the country now imports substantial amounts of crude petroleum from other parts of the world, particularly the Near East and the Caribbean area.

Crude petroleum imports from Arab countries are less important for the United States, however, than they are for most western European countries. If necessary the United States could get along without these imports. For most European countries, a drastic reduction of these imports would have disastrous economic consequences.

Another important source of energy is natural gas. A vast network of pipelines conducts this gas from the places where it is found to users in industrial centers and large urban agglomerations. Proved reserves of natural gas amounted to 275,109 billion cubic feet (7.79 billion m.^{3}) on 31 December, 1969.[15] In 1969 the production of natural gas was 20,698 billion cubic feet (0.59 billion m.^{3}). The most important producer states were Texas, Louisiana, Oklahoma, New Mexico, and Kansas.

Metal Mining

The United States produced 91.2 million tons of iron ore in 1970.[16] Though most of this ore (71.3 million tons) was mined in the Lake Superior regions, many of the richer iron ore deposits in Minnesota and Michigan have been exhausted. Nowadays recourse is taken to lower percentage ores that must first be concentrated in special processes before it is economically feasible to use them. Because the domestic production is no longer sufficient, the country has become a great importer of iron ores from Canada, Sweden, Venezuela, and Chile. Imports amount to 45.6 million tons in 1970. The domestic share in world production of iron ore was 12.1%.

Production of primary (new) copper from domestic ores amounted to 1.547 million tons in 1970. In the same year, 0.35 million tons of unmanufactured copper were imported and 0.24 million tons of refined copper exported.[17] In 1969 the production of copper smelters in the United States was 21% of the world total; the average for the years 1951–55 had been 28%. Copper ores are now mined mainly in the states of Arizona, Utah, Montana, New Mexico, and Nevada.

The country has to rely heavily on imports for some other important metals, such as nickel, lead, tungsten, and tin. The production of aluminum requires the import of large amounts of bauxite. On the other hand, production of metals like molybdenum and magnesium exceeds domestic consumption, so the country is a net exporter.

Domestic production of a large number of metals is considerable and could no doubt be stepped up if the need should arise. The country's share in the world production of some metals has decreased drastically between 1950 and 1970. In others its share has decreased moderately, and in yet others it has increased. Variations in the nation's share in world production are partly due to changes in technology and in domestic demand for the different metals. Partly they reflect economic expansion and increased industrialization in other countries, which entailed larger metals production.

Nonmetallic Minerals

Among the nonmetallic minerals we may single out four that are important basic raw products for the chemical industry: sulfur, phosphate rock, potash, and rock salt. In 1970 sulfur

TABLE 12

Production of Selected Minerals in the United States, the Soviet Union, West Germany, and the World in 1969

	United States	Soviet Union	West Germany	World Total	United States as % of World Total 1968 or 1969	1958*
Coal (mill. tn.)	514.1	425.8	111.6	2,036	25.3	21.4
Lignite (mill. tn.)	4.5	182.0	107.4	. . . . .	. . . . .	. . . . .
Raw Oil (mill. tn.)	510.0	353.0	7.5	. . . . .	22.0**	35.6
Natural Gas (mill m.³)	585.0	182.8	8.1	. . . . .	. . . . .	. . . . .
Iron Ores (mill. tn.) (Iron content)	52.6	97.0	2.0	387.90	13.6	18.1
Copper Ore (mill. tn.) (Copper content)	1.4	0.88	negl.	5.95	23.5	26.0
Lead Ore (1,000 tn.) (Lead content)	462	460	39	3,250	14.2	12.1
Zinc Ores (1,000 tn.) (Zinc content)	502	530	111	5,200	9.7	14.2
Pyrites (Schwefel-kies) (1,000 tn.) (1968)	886	. . . . .	616	22,085	4.0	6.8
Phosphates (1,000 tn.) (1968)	37,414	16,687	. . . . .	83,900	44.6	52.5
Bauxite (1,000 tn.) (1968)	1,825	5,200	. . . . .	55,000	3.3	7.2

Source: Statistisches Jahrbuch 1971, p. 61 to 65. All units are in metric tons, if not otherwise indicated.

*Calculated from *Statistisches Jahrbuch 1961,* p. 56 to 59.
**Source: Statistical Abstract 1971,* p. 644, table 1053. Computed from volume.

production in all forms amounted to 9.74 million tons; phosphate rock (P_2O_2 content), 16.3 million tons, and potash (K_2O content), 2.5 million tons. Rock salt production amounted to 40.1 million tons.[18] The country was a net importer of potash (2.1 million tons imports and 0.6 million tons exports, in 1970). For phosphate rocks and sulfur, the country was a net exporter. The amount of imported rock salt is small relative to domestic production.

Table 12 summarizes the mineral production of the

United States in 1969. For the sake of comparison, 1969 production figures for the Soviet Union, West Germany, and the world are also shown.

The Atmosphere

Until recently it was customary to assume that the air in the atmosphere was free, available in good quality in unlimited quantities. Modern technology and the contemporary way of living in large urban agglomerations have made this assumption questionable. With thousands of tons of fuels being burnt by individuals and enterprises each day, air pollution has become a major problem of some large American cities. Because of strong public demand for air pollution controls, special legislation has been enacted. The economic implications of such legislation, for instance, federal control over automobile exhaust emissions, are that special and often costly pollution control devices must be introduced in plants and new cars. As in all other modern industrialized nations, good fresh air is scarcely an unlimited free resource any longer in the United States.

Literature

Adelman, M.A. *The World Petroleum Market.* Baltimore: Johns Hopkins University Press, 1972.

Barnett, H.J., and Morse, C. *Scarcity and Growth.* Baltimore: Johns Hopkins University Press, 1963, 1965.

Darmstadter, J.; Teitlebaum, P.; and Polach, J. *Energy in the World Economy.* Baltimore: Johns Hopkins University Press, 1971.

Landsberg, H.; Fischman, L.; and Fisher, J. *Resources in America's Future.* Baltimore: Johns Hopkins University Press, 1963.

Potter, N., and Christy, F. *Trends in Natural Resource Commodities.* Baltimore: Johns Hopkins University Press, 1963.

U.S. Department of Agriculture. *Yearbook.* Washington, D.C.: U.S. Government Printing Office. Published annually.

U.S. Bureau of Mines. *Mineral Facts and Problems.* Bulletin 650. Washington, D.C.: U.S. Government Printing Office, 1970, 1291 p. See also *Minerals Yearbook.*

U.S. Commission on Population Growth and the American Future. *Population, Resources, and the Environment.* Vol. 3. Washington D.C.: U.S. Government Printing Office, 1972.

U.S. Council on Environmental Quality. *Third and Fourth Annual Reports.* Washington, D.C.: U.S. Government Printing Office, 1972, 1973.

U.S. President's Materials Policy Commission. *Resources for Freedom.* 5 vols. Washington, D.C.: U.S. Government Printing Office, 1952.

4.
Capital Stock

One of the best definitions of capital has been given by
Nobel Prize laureate Simon Kuznets in his book *Capital in
the American Economy.* He wrote: "In modern society capital is the stock of means separable from human beings and
legally disposable in economic transactions intended for use
in producing goods or income."[1] Capital thus defined is at
any time owned by various units in an economy. It takes the
form of tangible assets and intangible assets. Tangible assets
consist of land, structures, equipment, and inventories of
different kinds. Intangible assets are financial assets that
consist of domestic claims and claims against foreigners.
They form a claim structure which has the characteristic that
there is against any domestic financial asset an offsetting
obligation. Domestic claims, in the bookkeeping sense, can-
cel each other out, whereas positive and negative claims
against foreigners do not need to do so. If one wishes
to determine the total capital or wealth of a nation, one
must add tangible assets and net claims against foreigners.
In the analysis of production, capital is usually regarded as
the sum of tangible assets only. Claims against foreigners,
though important with respect to the possibility of obtaining
resources needed for production from abroad, are in this

context omitted. Following this tradition, we shall deal with tangible assets only.

The tangible assets of a nation can be analyzed as being either reproducible or nonreproducible. Reproducible assets are those which come into existence through the productive efforts of man; they can be created, changed, replaced, and destroyed. The total of all reproducible assets is conventionally referred to as the physical capital stock. Nonreproducible assets are those which are given to man by nature and which he cannot (save in rare instances) increase.

In industrialized nations, the largest part of national capital consists of man-made reproducible assets. Such assets take an immense variety of forms, from super highways, airfields, blast furnaces, machine tools, houses, hammers, down to tiny instruments. All are physical capital goods, existing at a certain time in a certain volume and structure determined by economic and technological considerations. Capital goods are heterogeneous. Each of them generally serves a limited number of purposes, has a specific lifetime, and embodies in itself a particular technology.[2] Because it would be very difficult to account for all these specific features, in economic theory economists have tried to aggregate, in some meaningful way, the various heterogeneous capital goods so as to obtain a numerical value of their total, the value of the capital stock.

In the following pages, figures will be presented on the American capital stock in dollar terms. In order to avoid a misunderstanding of these it is useful to deal briefly with a very old economic problem, the measurement of the capital stock and, related to it, the determination of the rate of return on capital, or the real rate of interest. During the last century many of the foremost economists have struggled with this problem, and there were several well-known controversies about it, but the problem still has not been solved.[3]

Capital goods are produced because it is expected that a net benefit can be derived from them. They are expected to "pay off." The decision to produce a capital good involves two considerations, its production cost and the benefits that can be derived from it. Because capital goods generally serve for several future time periods and no human being knows what the future will be, some degree of uncertainty attaches to the benefits from any capital good. If the investor wishes to know what is the present value of the sum of the future income stream that will emanate from the capital good, each item within the stream must be discounted properly. This is necessary to account for the fact that (a) since he obtains the incomes at future dates only, they will be worth less to him than equivalent present incomes and (b) that uncertainties surround future incomes. If the sum of the discounted future income stream should be smaller than the production cost of the capital good, the good will not be produced. Should it be larger than cost, its production is worthwhile. The matter seems to be simple.

The problem arises in determining the interest rate with which the future income stream is to be discounted. To indicate what is involved we consider the case of a perfectly competitive market economy in equilibrium. Such an economy is characterized by the absence of risk and uncertainty, which simplifies matters. In this economy the interest rate is equal to the rate of return on capital, or the real rate of interest, which in turn should equal—assuming the simplest case of a constant return to scale production function—the marginal productivity of capital. To determine the real rate of interest, however, one needs a production function with a given capital stock. Thus the dilemma arises: we cannot determine the capital stock if we do not know the real rate of interest, and we cannot determine the real rate of interest if we do not know the capital stock. It is therefore not possible to determine the size of the capital stock through the capitalization of incomes emanating from it.[4]

An alternate method of aggregating the various capital goods into a capital stock has therefore been used. It is called the "perpetual inventory" method. This method is based on the reproduction cost of various types of assets and requires several steps in the derivation of a real capital stock time series. The first step is to collect all figures on annual gross domestic capital expenditures by different types of capital goods. These expenditures are then deflated with appropriate construction cost or wholesale price indexes. The next step is to estimate the life span of the different types of capital goods, from which depreciation schedules can be derived. With the aid of these, the existing capital goods (at original cost prices) are depreciated in annual intervals. Thus one can determine net capital expenditures in each year which will equal gross capital expenditures, minus the sum of all depreciation of existing capital goods of different ages. The last step is to cumulate the net capital expenditures for as many years backwards as correspond to the lifetime of the particular types of capital goods involved. In this way one can synthetically build up a capital stock that consists of different layers, sometimes called "vintages," of capital goods, each embodying a particular technology.

This perpetual inventory method of determining the capital stock has several shortcomings, but there seems at the present time to be no better way to obtain an approximate measure of it. The figures on the U.S. capital stock presented below were derived by this method.

The capital stock of the United States, defined as the total of all tangible assets, grew during the last sixty-seven years at an average rate of approximately 2.5% a year. In 1900 it amounted to $315 billion and in 1967 to $1,676 billion, in 1947–49 constant prices.[5] The capital stock grew more rapidly than the population, thus increasing substantially the capital per capita. In 1900, capital per capita was $4,099 (in 1947–49 prices) and in 1967, $8,367. In both the production and consumer sector, American life became more capital-intensive. But the quantitative aspect is not all; the quality of the capital stock also improved, becoming much more productive. In 1900 there were 5.6 dollars of capital for each dollar of net national product (NNP); in 1967, only 3.7 dollars.[6]

Of special interest to the economist is the part of the

TABLE 13

Totals of Tangible Assets, Reproducible Assets, and Land, 1952–68
(In Billions of Dollars)

Year	Total Tangible Assets	Total Reproducible Assets	Land*	Total Reproducible Assets	Structures	All Other Reproducible Assets
	In current prices			In 1958 prices		
1952	1,115	916	199	1,025	642	383
1956	1,481	1,189	292	1,221	765	456
1960	1,851	1,440	411	1,394	893	501
1964	2,309	1,755	554	1,621	1,032	589
1965	2,475	1,881	594	1,701	1,072	629
1966	2,671	2,035	636	1,787	1,110	677
1967	2,869	2,193	676	1,849	1,142	707
1968	3,079	2,364	715	1,936	1,178	758

Source: Statistical Abstract, 1971, p. 328, table 524; p. 329, table 525 (rounded values, digits omitted). For capital stock figures for earlier years back to 1850 see U.S. Department of Commerce, *Historical Statistics, Colonial Times to 1957,* Washington, D.C., Series F. 222–46.

*Calculated as difference between total tangible and total reproducible assets.

capital stock that consists of reproducible assets, the whole collection of man-made capital goods ranging from huge buildings to minute instruments. The volume and structure of reproducible assets are of central importance for production and economic growth. The size of this capital stock is determined by the share of production that a nation devotes to investment and, possibly, by certain fortuitous or adverse extraneous events such as obtaining productive resources through nature's grace or—as is much more important in our world—destruction of productive resources through war. For the U.S. economy such extraneous events were negligible during the last seven decades. In this period the capital formation came out of current production and reflected the real savings of the nation. Outside events put few, if any, constraints on capital formation. Rapid capital formation in turn increased productivity, output, and incomes, from

TABLE 14

The Structure of Reproducible Assets, 1952–68
(In Billions of Dollars, 1958 constant prices)

Year	Total Repro-ducible Assets	Struc-tures (Total)	Equipment Pro-ducer Durables	Con-sumer Durables	Inventories Private Farm	Private Nonfarm	Public
1952	1,025	642	162	95	25	93	8
1956	1,221	765	195	124	19	103	16
1960	1,394	893	219	140	15	109	18
1964	1,621	1,032	252	169	23	128	17
1965	1,701	1,072	268	184	26	136	16
1966	1,787	1,110	288	199	27	150	12
1967	1,849	1,142	308	211	25	151	12
1968	1,936	1,178	327	227	27	164	13

Source: Statistical Abstract, 1971, p. 329, table 525 (rounded values; details may not add up to total).

which further savings could be made. Between 1900 and 1970, capital formation in the U.S. economy was, for any single country, the largest in the world. In 1968 the total of reproducible assets was estimated at $1,178 billion, in 1958 constant prices.

Of what types of assets does the American reproducible capital stock consist? It comprises structures—all kinds of buildings, roads, and other construction, equipment in both the producer and consumer sectors, and inventories. The bulk of all reproducible assets take the form of structures. They accounted for 60.8% of all reproducible assets in 1968. Equipment in the production sector consists of all types of machinery and facilities required for production. In the consumer sector, equipment comprises durable consumer goods, including cars and various types of labor-saving household appliances. Both equipment subgroups together accounted for 28.6% of all reproducible assets in 1968. Inventories, which consist of raw materials and semi-finished and finished goods, accounted for 10.5%. Further breakdowns as to who held the various types of assets can be found in tables 14 and 15. The largest single asset type

TABLE 15
*The Structure of the Capital Stock: Assets in Structures,
1952–68*
(In Billions of Dollars, 1958 Constant Prices)

| | | Nonfarm Structures | | | | |
Year	Structures Total	Public non-residential	Institu-tional	Other private non-residential	Residential	Farm Structures
1952	642	169	17	128	297	31
1956	765	202	21	150	357	35
1960	893	243	27	172	413	37
1964	1,032	293	35	195	472	37
1965	1,072	306	37	204	485	39
1966	1,110	321	40	214	497	39
1967	1,143	332	42	223	507	39
1968	1,178	344	44	232	519	40

*Source: Statistical Abstract, 1971, p. 329, table 525 (rounded values; details
may not add up to total).*

in the American economy is residential construction. It comprises the millions of homes of Americans. After this, in order
of importance, come public nonresidential construction, such
as roads, harbors, airfields, and public buildings; then durable equipment held by producers.

The "means of production," considered in the narrow
sense as "those which permit industrial production," can be
estimated from tables 14 and 15. If we add "producer durable
equipment" and "other private nonresidential construction"
(most of which are factories or buildings for commercial use)
we get a figure of $559 billion for 1968, which is only 28.9%
of the nation's total reproducible assets. This reveals an important fact: capital for industrial production, though of key
importance in the economy, must nowadays be supplemented by a substantial amount of public capital and capital
in the consumer sector in order to be effective. Such capital,
including "public nonresidential construction," "residential
construction," and "consumer durables," was equal to 56.3%
of all reproducible assets in 1968. It is productive too and has
the characteristics of other capital goods. Treating the two

types of capital as consumer goods, as it is done in some important respects in national income accounting and for taxation purposes, is not realistic.

Literature

Goldsmith, Raymond W. *The National Wealth of the United States in the Postwar Period.* Princeton, N.J.: Princeton University Press, 1962.

Kuznets, Simon, assisted by Elizabeth Jenks. *Capital in the American Economy: Its Formation and Financing.* A study by the National Bureau of Economic Research. Princeton, N.J.: Princeton University Press, 1961.

Tice, H. S. "Depreciation, Obsolescence and the Measurement of the Aggregate Capital Stock of the United States." *Review of Income and Wealth* (June 1967), pp. 119–54.

5.
The Intangible:
Technological Progress

To use labor, natural resources and capital effectively in the process of production requires technological knowledge. This type of knowledge has existed, in different degrees, in all societies and since the earliest times. Technological progress permits man to obtain more and better goods and services with less effort. It helps him to push back the constraints with which he is confronted in this world of scarcity. Technological progress occurs in many places, sometimes isolated, sometimes simultaneously. Indeed, inventions and discoveries seem to be a universal characteristic of mankind. Yet the speed of technological progress has varied greatly for different societies and time periods.

Some economists have argued that technological progress and innovation are the prime movers of a dynamic market economy in which consumers try to maximize utilities; and entrepreneurs, profits.[1] Entrepreneurs have good reasons to innovate. If they do it successfully they can expect to obtain excess profits, at least until imitation of the innovations by others overtake them. Technological progress and innovations at first generate benefits to those who take the risk of introducing them. Later on they benefit all.

It is not well understood what factors ultimately underlie technological progress. Though several hypotheses have been advanced, such as the "great man" theory, the deterministic sociological theory of inventions, and in-between versions of both, there seems to be no consensus as to how technological, social, psychological, and economic factors affect discoveries and inventions. Whatever its driving force, technological progress as the result of discoveries and inventions is nowadays of prime importance for economic growth in advanced economies. Some economists have argued that at least 20% of all increases in production of the United States economy can be attributed to technological progress.[2]

There is, however, no way to measure precisely the contribution of technological progress to production. It is sometimes inferred from an unexplained residual in aggregate production function estimates. The size of the residual depends, however, on the functional form of the estimated production function. In addition, the residual acts as a "catch-all" item and may reflect other influences. Further, there is the question: In what factor of production is technological progress embodied? Knowledge no doubt originates in human beings and might be called "human capital." Yet, part of this knowledge may be frozen into sophisticated capital goods. This raises considerable conceptual problems. Technological progress is an intangible factor that eludes quantitative measurement.

Instead of trying to detect what contribution technological knowledge made to production, it is therefore perhaps more useful to have a look at it from another point of view, that of input. What efforts did the American economy make, through education, research and development projects, and other activities to further technological developments in recent years?

Technological progress in our age is based largely on systematic scientific research. Because those who contribute to it have usually received advanced university training, we may start by tracing the supply of scientists at the university level.

In 1960 the total graduate enrollment in all fields was 314,349. Of these, 93,828 were in the science fields, exclusive of psychology and the social sciences. With the stress on economic growth and technological advances during the 1960s, total enrollment rose to 756,865 in 1969. Of these, 178,311 were in the science fields, exclusive of psychology and the social sciences. Mathematics, the physical sciences, and engineering registered strong enrollment increases. The number of doctorates conferred rose also. In mathematics, 291 doctorates were awarded in 1960; in 1970 there were 1,218. In engineering the number rose from 792 in 1960 to 3,432 in 1970, and in the physical sciences the increase was from 1,861 to 4,389.[3] These few figures indicate the important role American universities have in forming the abilities and talents on which technological progress largely depends.

According to statistics based on a voluntary registration by the National Science Foundation, there were 312,644 scientists, including economists and other social scientists, in 1970. Excluding these, the number was 281,880.[4] The actual number of scientists may have been larger; registration was voluntary. There were 253,536 scientists and engineers working in universities and colleges in January 1969.[5]

In spite of the prodigious domestic increases in U.S.-trained scientific personnel, the country continued to draw on manpower trained abroad. Historically the United States has always admitted scientists as immigrants. They have come to this country for a variety of reasons: political, sociological, economic, and scientific ones. Foreign-born and foreign-trained scientists have often made outstanding contributions to the nation's science and technology, the prime example being the large inflow of first-rate German scientists during Hitler's reign. Yet, loss of highly trained manpower is a serious matter for many countries. In the 1960s some foreign countries, especially Great Britain, complained bitterly about a damaging "brain drain" because of its loss of scientists to the United States. The total number of scientists and engineers admitted into the United States as immigrants was 67,400 between 1964 and 1970. Of these, 46,675 persons were engineers; 17,433, natural scientists. A good share of the U.S. technological progress has its roots in foreign efforts.

Another indicator of the furtherance of a nation's technological progress is the amount of financial resources it devotes to organized research. The expenditures for basic research, applied research, and development in the United States amounted to $6.28 billion in 1955. Of this, expenditures for basic research amounted to $0.608 billion, applied research accounted for $1.525 billion, and development for $4.146 billion.[6] These figures were at the time often mentioned with pride; yet they proved to be much too low, given rapid technological advances in other nations. The advent of the space age, with the spectacular Russian Sputnik success, led in the years after 1957 to considerable increases in U.S. research and development expenditures. In 1960 they amounted to $13.7 billion, and $26.85 billion in 1970. Many of the technological problems that arose required basic research, whose share of the total expenditures therefore rose from 9.6% in 1955 to 14.1% in 1970. It is still unknown whether this increase is large enough to sustain long-range technological progress.

The cost of basic research is often high, and private firms may be reluctant to undertake it if there is not a good prospect for a pay-off in the near future. If basic research is to be done, the government often has to support it. Much U.S. research has been defense- and space-related, though at a diminishing rate (48.4% in 1955 and 42.1% in 1970). The federal government has become heavily involved in research and development, either as a direct participant or a source of funds. Its share in the total expenditures rose from 55.9% in 1955 to a peak of 65.4% in 1964 (see table 16). Since then it has declined; it was only 54.9% in 1971.

TABLE 16

Research and Development Expenditures: Totals, Defense-
and Space-related, and Other Outlays, 1955-71 (In Billions
of Dollars, Current Prices)

Year	Total Research and Development	As % of Total Research and Development Expenditure				Sum of (2), (3) and (4)
		Defense-related	Space-related	Other Expenditure		
				Federal	Nonfederal	
	(1)	(2)	(3)	(4)	(5)	(6)
1955	6.28	47.4	1.0	7.5	44.1	55.9
1958	10.87	52.0	1.0	9.5	37.5	62.5
1961	14.55	49.2	5.5	9.0	36.3	63.7
1964	19.21	36.0	19.7	9.7	34.6	65.4
1967	23.64	31.7	18.0	11.4	38.9	61.1
1970	26.56	31.6	10.7	13.3	44.4	55.6
1971 (preliminary)	27.31	31.0	9.2	14.7	45.1	54.9

*Source: Statistical Abstract 1971, p. 508, table 800; further source: National
Science Foundation, National Patterns of R & D: Resources—Funds and
Manpower in the United States, 1953-71 (NSF 70–46).*

Industry is the second largest supplier of funds for research and development. It contributed 39.0% in 1971. The
remaining funds come from universities, colleges, and nonprofit institutions. The bulk of all basic research was done in
universities, with heavy financial support from the federal
government.

The man-years of work spent on research and development projects and the cost per scientist and engineer also
give an indication of the nation's efforts to further technological progress. In 1969 the number of man-years scientists and
engineers put into research and development projects was
383,000.[7] Approximately half of this work was performed in
the fields of electrical equipment and communication and
aircraft and missiles. Only 28.0% of all man-years were spent
in the more traditional fields of chemicals and allied products, machinery, and motor vehicles and other transportation
equipment. The average cost per scientist or engineer ranged
from $68,900 in the automotive and transportation field to

TABLE 17
Number of
Patents in the United States in 1960 and 1970

	1960	1970
Patent applications filed:	84,475	109,359
Inventions	79,590	102,868
Designs	4,525	5,996
Botanical plants	131	188
Reissues	229	307
Patents issued:	49,986	67,962
Inventions, total	47,170	64,427
Inventions by individuals	13,069	13,511
Inventions by U.S. corporations	28,187	36,896
Inventions by foreign corporations	4,670	12,294
Inventions by U.S. government	1,244	1,726
Designs	2,543	3,214
Botanical plants	116	52
Reissues	157	269
Others	. . . . .	215

Source: Statistical Abstract, 1971, p. 518, table 822.

$40,300 in the machinery field. The distribution of man-years mirrors the preponderance of defense- and space-related research.

Successful research and development work, at least as far as the nonmilitary sector is concerned, will often result in patent applications and patent issues. The purposes for which patents are issued vary widely, however, and there is no way to infer from their number what contributions were actually made to technological progress. Still, those issued give some idea about the volume and origin of inventions. Table 17 summarizes patent applications and issues in 1960 and 1970. The total number of patents issued was 67,962 in 1970, nearly 18,000 more than in 1960. Whereas the number of patents for inventions by individuals had risen slightly, those by domestic and foreign corporations increased substantially, reflecting the recent upsurge of company-sponsored research and, one stage further removed, the need to innovate and to be progressive in a market economy.

In the long run, the welfare of the nation, as well as its security, depends critically on technological knowledge; this is nowadays fully recognized. To keep it at a high level, considerable resources were made available in the period after World War II. With such spectacular achievements as several manned landings on the moon and putting a satellite in orbit around the planet Mars, it seemed that American technological know-how was still in the lead in the early seventies. Yet, formidable competitors in other parts of the world have appeared, ready to challenge this lead in the future.

6.
Production of the Economy

The Development of Gross National Product between 1929 and 1970

The product of a nation consists of a large number of different goods and services which are incommensurable and cannot be added directly. The need to obtain a useful measure of total production and the incomes generated thereby led to the development of national income statistics, which are now readily available for the United States and many other countries.[1] We shall use these data to trace the development of production in the United States during the last decades. The best known national income aggregate is gross national product (GNP), which equals the total national output of goods and services, valued at market prices. Today the GNP is closely watched by economists, politicians, businessmen, and other citizens. Its subaggregates, net national product, national product, personal income, disposable personal income, and personal savings, provide additional information on the economy.

To trace the development of American production it is

useful to choose a time period long enough to cover several major changes and recent enough that the lessons learned in it are still relevant for the present. We shall therefore start our analysis with the fateful year 1929, which ushered in the Great Depression.

The GNP amounted to $103.1 billion in current and $203.6 billion in 1958 constant prices in 1929. The Great Depression brought sharp declines in production and incomes in the United States as well as in other major industrialized countries. When the world economic crisis culminated, the American GNP had fallen to 69.5% of its 1929 value. In 1933 it was down to $55.6 billion in current prices and $141.5 billion in 1958 constant prices. These figures speak for themselves. An economic disaster had struck the country. There was large-scale unemployment, and many productive capacities were idle; the nation was using only a fraction of its productive resources. The social cost—huge losses in income, widespread human misery—was staggering. And this state of affairs was not quickly overcome. It took four years to reach the bottom of the Depression and more than six years to pull out of it, despite various government measures to speed up recovery. Only in 1939–40 did production and incomes again reach the 1929 level. It is sometimes said that the enormous economic losses of the Great Depression were equal to the country's total war effort during World War II.

The experience of this period was so shattering as to leave a deep imprint in people's minds. The Great Depression raised serious questions about the alleged ability of a market economy to achieve at all times a high level of resource use by quickly overcoming departures from such full use. Orthodox classical economic theory had taught that this should occur; yet the reality was different. A deep skepticism arose about the tenets of conventional economic theory. At the same time there was a desire to find a remedy for the social misery of unemployment. A new economic theory set forth by the English economist John Maynard Keynes in

1935 seemed to have the answers to the problems at hand and therefore caused much interest. His book *The General Theory of Employment Interest and Money* was destined to profoundly influence economic theory and policy in the United States during the decades to come.[2]

By the time World War II started in Europe, the American real GNP was back at the 1929 level, yet the rate of U.S. unemployment remained high. In 1940, 8.1 million people were still without work. World War II changed this state of affairs. When the country became a belligerent power in 1941, production was switched from goods for civilian use to materials needed for war. The need to supply the armed forces and provide aid to allied powers resulted in a substantial increase in production. In 1944 the real GNP reached the $361.3 billion mark, approximately twice its 1930 value. More and more people were absorbed in the productive process, and in 1945 the rate of unemployment hit a record low of 1.0%. This production was largely propelled by the demand for war-related materials, however, and the question arose as to how the economy would fare once the cessation of hostilities brought an end to this demand. Many economic experts predicted a substantial decline in economic activity and high postwar unemployment.

During the war, government expenditures had propelled the economy, but after 1945 these decreased. Everything else the same, aggregate demand might have fallen drastically. What the pessimistic forecasts overlooked was the extent of pent-up civilian demand. Since consumers could not obtain many of the goods they desired during the war, they built up savings. Once the war ended and more private goods became available again, consumers were eager to buy, so there was an upsurge in consumer demand. In addition to this came deferred-investment spending by firms. The rising private demand created considerable inflationary pressures, but it also caused production to remain high. Contrary to some predictions, the economy did not slide back to low, prewar levels of production. Admittedly, the years 1945–47 were difficult ones. The economy had to readjust to peace-time conditions.

A remarkable new phenomenon could be observed in this postwar period, however. Whereas in the 1930s declines in production had engendered declines in prices, the first postwar years showed *declines* in production with concomitant *increases* in prices. This indicated that important structural and behavioral changes had taken place in the economy. Henceforth prices were inflexible downward but flexible upward.

From 1949 on, production increased again, partly stimulated by the demand-pull due to the Korean war. This upswing lasted until the recession of 1953–54, which was of short duration. The recession of 1957–58 though painful for certain sectors of the economy, was also only an interlude. Still, both recessions in the 1950s marred the expansion of the economy; incomes were lost and adverse expectations were generated. Prices continued to rise, but at a more moderate rate than in the 1940s.

In 1959 there began for the American economy an unprecedented expansion period that lasted for more than a decade. During this period the real GNP increased from $475.9 billion to $727.1 billion. The average growth rate between 1960 and 1969 climbed to 4.5%, which compared very favorably with an average rate of only 2.1% between 1945 and 1961. It seemed that a breakthrough had finally occurred and that the economy had settled on a path to higher growth.

The rapid economic growth was, however, accompanied by a number of problems that put great stress on American society. In the second half of the 1960s an expansion of the war in Vietnam occurred, to which an increasingly large section of the population was bitterly opposed. More and more resources had to be sacrificed for this war. Concomitantly, there was a commitment by the Johnson administration to work towards a "great society," which involved substantial government outlays for social programs, many of which were designed to help the poor and underprivileged.

With high levels of employment and strained national resources, these additional programs led to budgetary deficits,
which in turn generated inflationary pressures. Often wages
and prices chased each other and rose more than the annual
increases in productivity. In this general setting a feeling
of malaise developed. Protests against the war in Vietnam
intensified; they were accompanied by racial strife. Many
Americans were disappointed by political and economic developments. There developed among them a feeling that a
rapid increase in aggregate real income was not necessarily
the only desirable social goal. By the end of the 1960s, the
nation's preferences and priorities seemed to have changed.
Economic policy henceforth laid less emphasis upon output
growth and full employment; attention was more and more
directed towards a dampening of inflationary pressures and
the distortions caused by them. A reasonable price level stability got first priority, and policy measures were taken to
achieve it. In the wake of these, the real GNP temporarily
ceased to grow. It fell slightly from $727.1 billion in 1969 to
$724.1 billion in 1970 (both figures in 1958 prices).[3] The
decrease in real GNP did not put a stop to price increases.

     This highly condensed account of the development of
GNP between 1929 and 1970 cannot take into account all the
historical details that are so minutely discussed by business
cycle experts and students of economic policy. Furthermore,
it should be kept in mind that GNP, on which we focused our
attention, is a very large aggregate; to understand fully what
was going on in the economy one has to look at its composition. Yet, the time series of the real GNP and of the implicit
GNP price deflator do reveal many things.

     First, production and incomes have been rising, but
with interruptions. Secondly, production and incomes were
much more stable after World War II than in the years before
it; since 1939 there has been a steady economic expansion
interrupted only by minor recessions, none of them remotely
comparable to the disaster of the thirties. The rates of expansion varied, however. Largely war-propelled in the 1940s,

they were on the average at a moderate level in the 1950s. They increased substantially during the 1960s, when the fear that the economy could only perform at a "stagnation growth rate" vanished.[4]

The expansion of GNP occurred within the framework of a market economy. In it the price mechanism and the interplay of market forces are supposed to achieve an optimal and efficient allocation of resources and to galvanize growth. In order for the price mechanism to perform properly, prices should be flexible, both upward and downward. The implicit GNP price deflator in table 18 shows, however, what happened to the price level and, one stage further removed, to all the price components of which it was made up during the period considered. Since 1939 prices have risen. There has been a continued inflation. The speed of this inflation varied; in some years it was low, in others high. According to the GNP price deflator, prices increased by more than 6% in 1969–70. High rates of inflation endanger the working of a dynamic market economy, jeopardizing the growth of production and real incomes.

The conflict between a high rate of economic growth, which should for social reasons be full-employment growth, and price level stability so far remains unsolved in the contemporary American economy. The same is true for many other market economies.

Origin of National Product by Economic Sectors

The U.S. GNP originates in four sectors: business, households and institutions, government, and the rest of the world. Of these the business sector contributes the largest part to GNP; it is followed by the government sector. Third is the household sector, which comprises private households and nonprofit institutions. The smallest contribution is made by the sector labelled "rest of the world." The products of

TABLE 18

*Gross National Product and Implicit Gross
National Product Price Deflators, 1929–70
(In Billions of Dollars, Current and 1958 Constant Prices)*

Year	Gross National Product Current Prices	Gross National Product, 1958 Constant Prices	Implicit Gross National Product Price Deflator	
			1958=100	1929=100*
1929	103.1	203.6	50.6	100.0
1930	90.4	183.5	49.3	97.4
1931	75.8	169.3	44.8	88.5
1932	58.0	144.2	40.2	79.4
1933	55.6	141.5	39.3	77.7
1934	65.1	154.3	42.2	83.4
1935	72.2	169.5	42.6	84.2
1936	82.5	193.0	42.7	84.4
1937	90.4	203.2	44.5	87.9
1938	84.7	192.9	43.9	86.8
1939	90.5	209.4	43.2	85.4
1940	99.7	227.2	43.9	86.8
1941	124.5	263.7	47.2	93.3
1942	157.9	297.8	53.0	104.7
1943	191.6	337.1	56.8	112.2
1944	210.1	361.3	58.2	115.0
1945	211.9	355.2	59.7	118.0
1946	208.5	312.6	66.7	131.8
1947	231.3	309.9	74.6	147.4
1948	257.6	323.7	79.6	157.3
1949	256.5	324.1	79.1	156.3
1950	284.8	355.3	80.2	158.4
1951	328.4	383.4	85.6	169.2
1952	345.5	395.1	87.5	172.9
1953	364.6	412.8	88.3	174.5
1954	364.8	407.0	89.6	177.1
1955	398.0	438.0	90.9	179.6
1956	419.2	446.1	94.0	185.8
1957	441.1	452.5	97.5	192.7
1958	447.3	447.3	100.0	197.6
1959	483.7	475.9	101.6	200.8
1960	503.7	487.7	103.3	204.2
1961	520.1	497.2	104.6	206.7
1962	560.3	529.8	105.8	209.1
1963	590.5	551.0	107.2	211.9
1964	632.4	581.1	108.8	215.2
1965	684.9	617.8	110.9	219.2
1966	747.6	657.1	113.8	224.9
1967	793.9	675.2	117.6	232.4
1968	865.0	707.2	122.3	241.7
1969	931.4	727.1	128.1	253.2
1970	976.5	724.1	134.9	266.6

Sources: For the years 1929–66: *Economic Report of the President, January 1969,* (Washington, D.C.: U.S. Government Printing Office, 1969), pp. 227, 228; for the years 1967–70: *Statistical Abstract 1971,* pp. 305, 306.

*Rebased to 1929 equal to 100.

GROSS NATIONAL PRODUCT AND PERSONAL CONSUMPTION EXPENDITURES, 1951–70.

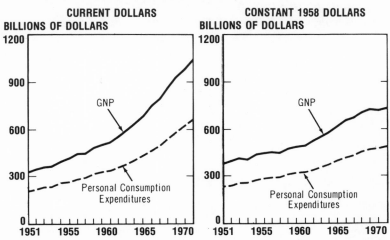

Fig. 5. Chart prepared by U.S. Bureau of Census. Data from U.S. Council of Economic Advisers. Reproduced from *Statistical Abstract 1972*, p. 311.

CONSUMER PRICE INDEXES, 1955–71 (1967 EQUALS 100).

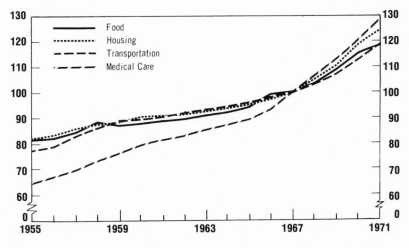

Fig. 6. Chart prepared by U.S. Bureau of Census. Data from U.S. Bureau of Labor Statistics. Reproduced from *Statistical Abstract 1972*, p. 341.

TABLE 19
Relation between Gross National Product and
National Income in 1969
(In Billions of Dollars, Current Prices)

	Aggregate:	
	Gross National Product	931.4
minus:	Capital Consumption Allowances	78.9
equals:	Net National Product	852.5
minus:	Indirect Business Taxes and	
	Nontax Liability	85.2
	Business Transfer Payments	3.5
	Statistical Discrepancy	−4.7
plus:	Net Subsidies of Government	
	Enterprises	1.0
equals:	National Income	769.5

Source: Statistical Abstract 1971, p. 309, table 492.

business, households and institutions, and the rest of the world are sometimes aggregated into gross private product. This aggregation is useful if the mixed character of the U.S. economy is to be brought into focus. The bulk of all production occurs in the private sector, but it is supplemented and complemented by production in the public sector.

There have been a number of studies on the growth of the public sector in market economies. Some have attempted to test the hypothesis of German scholar Adolph Wagner known as Wagner's Law, which asserts that in modern market economies public sector activities will grow more rapidly than those in the private sector.[5] Public sector activities refer in this context usually to government expenditures and not to the income originating in the public sector. Table 20, which shows a few figures on the origin of the U.S. GNP for 1929–70, indicates that the public sector's share did expand relative to the private one, but the private sector still remains by far the largest.

The massive role of business in turning out the nation's product is evident from table 20. Nearly 85% of the GNP was produced by business in 1970.

TABLE 20

Origin of Gross National Product by Economic Sectors,
1929–70
(Percentage Distribution)

	1929	1940	1950	1960	1970
Business	92.2	89.4	90.0	87.5	84.8
Households and Institutions	2.8	2.4	2.2	2.6	3.1
Rest of the World	.8	.4	.4	.5	.5
Subtotal: Private Sector Combined	95.8	92.2	92.6	90.6	88.4
Government	4.2	7.8	7.3	9.4	11.6
Total Economy	100.0	100.0	100.0	100.0	100.0

Source: Calculated from *Statistical Abstract 1971,* "Gross National Product in Current Prices," p. 305, table 484.

Business Enterprises

For the understanding of the functioning of the U.S. economy, a knowledge of the structure and activities of its business enterprises is indispensable.

According to tax statistics, the country had 11.672 million businesses in 1968.[6] The majority of these, 9.212 million, were owned by single proprietors. Single proprietorship was, in 1968, still widespread in agriculture (3.206 million), in retail trade (1.623 million), and in the service sector (2.390 million).

Single proprietor firms are usually, but not necessarily, small ones. The owners often have a limited amount of capital, and they work in their own establishments. Small and medium-sized farms, gasoline stations, automotive repair shops, cleaning businesses, small restaurants, drugstores, hardware stores, bakeries, grocery stores, and service establishments are examples of this type of enterprises.

The economic fate of these enterprises is often beset with uncertainty, however, in view of keen competition from

many (sometimes too many) similar businesses in the immediate neighborhood (street crossings with gasoline stations on
all four corners are perhaps the most visible example) and
competition from larger partnership firms or corporations. Yet
thousands of enterprising men and women try their luck at
being entrepreneurs and establish new firms each year, often
working long hours to succeed, frequently for a return that is
below what they could earn in a wage- or salary-paying position. A desire to be independent is no doubt in these cases an
important motivating force, but riding the wide and sometimes stormy ocean of the American economy in the small
boat of a limited-resource, single-proprietorship firm is risky.

Too low a volume of business and insufficient profits
are the perils of the small American business enterprise. In
1968, 60% of all single proprietorship firms had less than
$10,000 in annual gross receipts; and 78.2% had less than
$25,000.[7] The average net profit (after deductions of losses)
for all single proprietorship firms was only $3,459 in 1968.
Agriculture had the lowest average net profit, with $1,105,
and service establishments the highest, with $5,709.[8]

Small business firms are a familiar feature of the
American economic landscape. They perform important functions and help to maintain an adequate economic structure at
the local level. In an economy marked by the efficiency and
uniformity of mass production, much of what Americans
cherish is still found in small enterprises: individuality, en-
trepreneurship, and the drive to achieve and succeed, even if
the odds for success are not too favorable. Yet, the fate of this
type of enterprise is uncertain. Considering the large amount
of capital funds needed to acquire modern equipment and to
produce efficiently, it is likely that in the long run small
business will maintain itself only in those sectors where particularly individual abilities and skills are indispensable.

About 7.9% of all business enterprises were partnerships in 1968. This type of ownership form is found essentially in four types of industries: agriculture; retail trade;
finance, insurance, and real estate; and the service industry.

These industries comprised 84% of all partnerships in 1968. Partnerships in most cases dispose of more capital than single proprietorship business; the sales volume is larger and profits are higher. The average amount of gross business receipts was $87,725 and the average net profit (after deduction of losses), $12,424 in 1968.[9] Average profits varied widely, however, ranging from $3,572 for partnerships in finance, insurance, and real estate to $33,085 for firms in the service industry. Being somewhat larger, partnerships can usually weather adverse economic conditions better than single-proprietorship firms. They are, however, beset with well-known weaknesses. It may be difficult to find desirable partners to start a firm. Later on, the leaving of one partner may put the whole enterprise in jeopardy. In any case, this form of business does not seem to have had much appeal in the 1960s. The number of active partnerships diminished from 941,000 in 1960 to 918,000 in 1968.

The most important type of American business enterprise, in terms of business receipts and net profits, is the corporation. Incorporation has several important advantages. It is easier for a corporation to raise capital than for other types of enterprises, partly because of easier access to capital markets; and the life of the corporation is independent of that of its shareholders, whose responsibility is generally limited to the value of their shares. Becoming a shareholder in a company whose stock is traded on a stock exchange is as simple a matter as buying or selling that particular stock. The corporate form is a desirable one for firms with large capital requirements. Conditions for incorporation in the United States are not too stringent—they are much less so than in some European countries. Thus this form of enterprise is also often chosen for relatively small businesses, which explains the large number of corporations. In 1939 there were 470,000 corporations, but this total increased to 1.542 million in 1968.[10]

Corporations can be found in all sectors of the U.S. economy. In 1968 the largest number were in the finance,

TABLE 21

Proprietorships, Partnerships, and Corporations

Year	Number (1000s)	Proprietor-ships	Partner-ships	Active Corporations	All Business Forms
		Percentage Distribution of Numbers			
1945	6,737	84.4	9.3	6.2	100.0
1960	11,172	81.3	8.4	10.2	100.0
1965	11,416	79.5	8.0	12.5	100.0
1968	11,672	78.9	7.9	13.2	100.0
Receipts (in billions of dollars)		Percentage Distribution of Receipts*			
1945	382	20.7	12.3	66.9	100.0
1960	1,095	15.6	6.8	77.6	100.0
1965	1,469	13.5	5.1	81.3	100.0
1968	1,813	12.2	4.6	83.2	100.0
Net Profits (in billions of dollars)		Percentage Distribution of Net Profits**			
1945	40	30.0	17.5	52.5	100.0
1960	73	28.8	11.0	60.2	100.0
1965	111	25.0	8.9	66.1	100.0
1968	129	24.8	8.5	66.7	100.0

Source: Computed from: *Statistical Abstract 1971*, p. 459, table 710.

*Receipts from sales and services, less rebates and returns, without capital gains or losses. Excludes income not associated with taxpayer's business.
**After deduction of losses.

insurance, and real estate industries (407,000). In retail trade there were 315,000 and in the service industry, 229,000 corporations. Manufacturing ranked fourth, with 192,000 corporations.[11]

The corporate sector has been growing since the end of World War II, as table 21 reveals. In 1968, corporations received 83.2% of all receipts and realized 66.7% of all net profits. Corporations with receipts in excess of $500,000 accounted for 91.4% of all corporate receipts.[12]

The largest part of all business is done, however, by the very large corporations. Private studies sometimes refer to the 500 largest industrial corporations as the core of the

American economy, but this number is arbitrary.[13] Official data on the concentration of corporate manufacturing assets and profits estimate the number of corporations in manufacturing at 202,710 in the period January-March 1970.[14] Of these, 200,000 had less than $10 million in assets. On the other hand, each of the largest 609 corporations had more than $100 million in assets. At the top were 102 corporations, each with more than one billion dollars in assets.

The 609 largest corporations held 75% of all assets in the manufacturing corporate sector and realized 82% of its net profits. The top 102 corporations held 48% of all assets and realized 53% of all profits. In 1960 there were only 28 manufacturing corporations with over one billion dollars in assets. They held 27% of all assets and realized 38% of all net profits. Concentration of assets and profits has thus continued at a fairly rapid rate.

The problem of large corporations and the concentration of economic power associated with them has long standing in American economic history. Defenders of large corporations have argued that size by itself is not objectionable. Indeed, innovative firms in a dynamic market economy characterized by the presence of risk and uncertainty may need to be of a certain size to fulfill their function properly. Yet it is also true that gigantic firms, possessing considerable market power, fit badly into the framework of a competitive market economy—as do giant trade unions. They are scarcely the "price takers" in competitive markets who must accept whatever those markets dictate, something that neoclassical economic theory prescribes as a precondition for an optimal market solution. If large corporations do have market power, what guarantee is there that they will use it to attain not only corporate objectives, but also those of the society in which they conduct their business? This is an important, albeit unanswered, question.[15]

So far, the role of the large corporation in the American economy and society has not been fully explored, understood, or defined. The problem is a delicate one that involves the reexamination of some basic premises of a modern capitalistic market economy.

Production by Industries, 1950–70.

A nation's production occurs in industries which are, to varying degrees, interrelated. Some use as inputs the outputs of others; some produce intermediate goods, some final goods; and others produce both. The way in which industries contribute to the total product of a nation is called the structure of production. It is the result of a large number of economic forces and changes over time. The advent of new technologies leads to adjustments in existing cost structures. Product innovations take place and the tastes of consumers change. This in turn may decrease the demand for one industry's product, whereas that of another rises. There will always be growing, mature, and declining industries.

The historical changes in the structure of production of western industrialized nations are well known. In the first phase of the transformation process from an agricultural to an industrial economy, agriculture's share in total production decreases. The resources released by agriculture are absorbed by manufacturing industries, where production rapidly increases. A large part of all services is, at the same time, still performed in households. At a later stage of the economic development process, more and more services are sold in the market. Increasing incomes lead to a demand for more and better services, and as a result the service sector grows. These long-run changes have been observed in many countries.

Recent changes in the structure of production of the American economy are in accordance with those predicted for an industrial nation. The data in table 22 indicate that the share of agriculture (including forestry and fisheries) in national income declined during the last decades: in 1929 it was still 9.5%; by 1950 it was down to 7.3%; and in 1970 it

TABLE 22

National Income by Industries,
Selected Years, 1950–70
(In Billions of Dollars, Current Prices)

Year	Nat. Income Billion $ Current Prices	% Nat. Income from Industry										Total Nat. Income
		Agric., Forestry, Fisheries	Mining & Construction	Mfg.	Transportation	Communications & Utilities	Wholesale & Retail Trade	Finance, Insurance, Real Estate	Services	Gov't & Gov't Enterprises	Rest of World	
	(1)	(2)	(3)	(4)	(5)	(6)	(7)	(8)	(9)	(10)	(11)	(12)
1950	241.1	7.3	7.1	31.6	5.6	3.0	17.0	9.1	9.0	9.8	.5	100.0
1955	331.0	4.7	6.8	32.6	4.8	3.6	15.8	10.3	9.4	11.5	.5	100.0
1960	414.5	4.1	6.4	30.3	4.4	4.1	15.5	11.1	10.7	12.8	.6	100.0
1965	559.0*	3.7	6.2	30.6	4.1	4.0	14.9	11.0	11.4	13.3	.7	100.0
1968	712.7	3.1	6.0	29.9	3.8	3.9	14.9	10.9	12.1	14.7	.7	100.0
1970	800.8	3.1	6.2	27.6	3.8	3.9	15.2	11.1	13.0	15.6	.6	100.0

Source: Statistical Abstract, 1971, p. 311, table 495.

*National income figure for 1965 is from U.S. Department of Commerce, Office of Business Economics, *The National Income and Product Accounts of the United States, 1929–1965* (Washington, D.C., 1966), pp. 21, 93.

had dwindled to a mere 3.1%. The relative share of manufacturing also declined. It was 31.6% in 1950 and 27.6% in 1970.
The service sector on the other hand expanded. Service industries can be defined as industries which do not transform,
transport, or trade material goods. Under this definition the
following industries make up the United States service sector:
the industry of finance, insurance, and real estate; the service
industry proper; and the largest part of the government sector.
In these industries originated 27.9% of national income in
1950 and 39.7% in 1970. Agriculture (including forestry and
fisheries), mining, construction, and manufacturing accounted
for only 36.9% of national income in 1970. Transport, trade,
and communications generated 22.9% of national income.
Transactions with the rest of the world accounted for 0.6%.
Thus a substantial part of production occurs nowadays in the
service sector as defined above. In it nearly two-fifths of the
American national income is earned.

The official national income statistics list more than
eighty industries, with twenty-two in manufacturing alone. It
would require a detailed study far beyond the scope of this
book to describe this complex interrelated industrial structure. We must content ourselves with a discussion of the
main economic sectors.

The figures below pertain to 1965—the last year for
which, at the time of writing, full information on national
income by industries was available.

In that year the U.S. national income amounted to
$559 billion. Its production required the efforts of 71.2 mil-
lion people. Of these, 68 million were full-time or part-time
employees, the rest, 3.2 million, were owners working in
their enterprises. The number of full-time equivalent employees was 62.8 million. A comparison of the number of
full-time equivalent employees and the average number of
full-time and part-time employees shows that part-time employment varied considerably from industry to industry. It
was low in agriculture, mining, manufacturing, transportation, the communication industry, and the utilities. On the

other hand, in trade, finance, and the service industry proper, part-time employment was high. Even the public sector had many part-time employees. Steady full-time employment thus seems to be a characteristic of industries with longer production planning periods. Trade and industries which provide services of various kinds may experience sharper seasonal fluctuations in demand, and they can often offer additional part-time employment.

The average annual pre-income tax earnings per full-time employee in all industries was $5,705 in 1965. Averages for different industries varied considerably, however. It was only $2,030 in agriculture, whereas in transportation it was $7,473. (We abstract from the very high $9,000 average earnings of 4,000 people in the "rest of the world" sector.) For 18 million full-time employees in manufacturing, average annual earnings were $6,386. In the trade and service sector, earnings were below the national average.

For the economy as a whole the wage share (sum of wages and salaries before income taxes divided by national income) was 70.3%, and nonwage income 29.7%, in 1965. The division of national income between wages and salaries on the one hand and nonwage income on the other is nowadays a common practice, because of its social significance. This division, however, presents conceptual problems. From table 23 it can be seen that nonwage income does contain a payment for the work of business owners, especially in agriculture, trade, and the service industry. To obtain a more accurate estimate of the "actual" wage share, one would have to impute the wages for owners of businesses, deduct these from nonwage incomes, and add them to wages and salaries. Wages and salaries are, for instance, much higher in agriculture than is reflected by its 16.8% in table 23. On the other hand, the 100% wage share shown in the same table for the public sector is also misleading. It is the result of a usage in U.S. national income accounting not to attribute a net productivity to the capital goods in the public sector.

Though these shortcomings of the wage-share data

TABLE 23

National Income, Employment, Average Annual Earnings per Full-time Employee and Wage Share by Industries in 1965

	National Income Dollars (Billion)	Number of Persons Engaged in production (Millions)	Number of Full-time Equiv. Employees (Millions)	Average Number of Full-time and Part-time Employees (Millions)	Average Annual Earnings per Full-time Employee (Dollars)	Wages and Salaries as % of National Income*
Agriculture, Forestry and Fisheries	21.028	4.039	1.661	1.679	2030	16.8
Mining	6.432	.670	.636	.636	6783	74.9
Construction	28.328	3.971	3.201	3.201	6593	81.1
Manufacturing	170.408	18.443	18.088	18.088	6386	76.3
Transportation	22.926	2.486	2.304	2.537	7473	83.2
Communication	11.152	.875	.871	.881	6618	58.4
Utilities (electric, gas, and sanitary services)	11.605	.638	.626	.626	7291	45.1
Wholesale and Retail trade	83.600	13.129	10.885	12.729	5436	75.5
Finance, Insurance and Real Estate	61.019	3.084	2.764	3.029	6070	30.9
Services	63.013	11.770	9.636	11.360	4292	69.0
Government and Government Enterprises	75.243	12.139	12.139	13.242	5701	100.0
Rest of the World	4.266	.004	.004	.004	9000	.1
Total for All Industries	559.020	71.248	62.815	68.012	5705	70.3

Source: The National Income and Product Accounts of the United States, 1929–65, pp. 21, 93, 101, 105, 109, 113.

*Computed from data given in The National Income and Product Accounts of the United States, 1929–1965, pp. 21 and 93.

must be kept in mind, they still reveal the differences in the labor intensity of production in the various industries. Shifts in demand from products produced by industries with low labor intensity to those with high labor intensity will increase employment, and vice versa. These shifts may also affect prices. In an economy characterized by downward price inflexibility and upward flexibility they may generate inflationary pressures.

The analysis of the industries in which production occured and where Americans earned their incomes in 1965 in terms of large aggregates should not let us forget the micro units, the firms and households of which the aggregates are made up. In the private sector, these are the decision-making units. According to conventional economic theory, owners of producing firms try to maximize profits—if not short-term profits then long-term ones—and consuming households try to maximize the benefits from a collection of goods and services they can buy with their incomes. The maximization processes are supposed to assure the most efficient use of productive resources and the highest level of consumer satisfaction in a competitive market economy. Yet the maximizations are subject to constraints. Of these the most important ones are disposable resources of the producing or consuming units. Available resources depend in turn on the income and property distribution in an economy. The income distribution tells us for whom production occurred. The property distribution shows what capital formation was possible over time for different units in the economy. The next chapter will be devoted to these important characteristics of the American economy.

7.
Income
Distribution

The income of a nation is distributed in various ways, between factors of production, persons, ethnological groups, the sexes, the young and the old, and regions. Of greatest interest for the economist are the functional and personal income distributions. The former informs us what income shares different factors of production received; the latter shows the incomes of persons in different income brackets. We shall discuss three income distributions in the U.S. economy: functional, personal, and regional.

The Functional Distribution of Income

In a market economy, factors of production are owned privately. The owners will make them available for productive purposes if it pays to do so. They must be adequately rewarded in terms of a share of the product produced. From empirical studies it is known how the total product of a nation is distributed between the factors of production.

Historically, one of the main tasks of economic analysis has been to rationalize and explain observed income distributions between factors of production. The factors interact or "function," production takes place, and concomitantly income is generated. If the distribution of income is solely determined by production, the resulting income distribution is referred to as "functional." The analysis is a macro-economic one if the factors of production and the income generated are large aggregates.

In the history of economic analysis several macro-income distribution theories have been advanced. The most important ones, as far as their impact on economic theory and policy is concerned, stem from the eighteenth and nine-teenth centuries and are contained in the works of François Quesnay, David Ricardo, Karl Marx, Philip Henry Wicksteed, J. B. Clark, and others. The efforts to formulate macro-income distribution theories have continued up to the present time.

From all macro-income distribution theories, the neo-classical marginal productivity theory still has the greatest appeal for many contemporary economists. If one accepts its basic assumptions (a linear homogeneous production func-tion, perfect competition, given quantities of factors of pro-duction), the theory links the production and distribution in a market economy. The functional income distribution is deter-mined by the contributions the different factors of production make to production. The per-unit price of each factor of pro-duction (e.g., the real wage rate for labor and the real rate of return on capital) is equal to its marginal physical product. Multiplying this factor price times the number of factor units used gives the total real income of that particular factor. Fi-nally, the sum of all factor incomes will just exhaust the pro-duct—a mathematical necessity according to Euler's theorem on linear homogenous functions, which underlies the margi-nal productivity theory. This is an elegant theoretical ap-proach to a rather complex problem and has not failed to intrigue generations of economists.

Many students have, however, questioned the rele-vance and usefulness of the marginal productivity theory as an explanation for observed income distributions. It is argued that a theory is only as good as the assumptions on which it rests. If the stipulated macro-economic production function—whose existence is usually tacitly assumed—does not possess the necessary functional properties, if the economy is characterized by imperfect competition, and if factor supplies are changing, the marginal productivity theory is not very helpful.

There are other difficulties on an empirical level that may be briefly indicated. Economic theory usually assumes that factors of production are identifiable as distinct productive inputs and that to each factor accrues a specific factor payment. This leads to statistical problems. If, for instance, somebody works for his own account, using his own capital, as is the case of proprietors, his income consists partly of a return to capital and partly of labor income. The problem gets even more difficult if the concept of capital is broadened to include "human capital," the formation and maintenance of which requires valuable scarce resources in the same way the formation of tangible capital does. From the functional point of view, labor income should then be split into labor income proper and a return to human capital.[1] Statistics presently available do not permit such separations. Available statistical aggregates often refer to hybrid factors. This obscures the actual functional income distribution and may lead to a wrong impression of changes therein.

At present no theory exists that can satisfactorily explain observed macro-income distributions. In modern, mixed economies these are evidently not only determined by economic factors but also by sociological, political, and technological ones.

The developments in the functional income distribution of the U.S. economy during the period 1929–69 are summarized in table 24. Shown are percentage distributions of national income by type of income. From these one must infer to what factor of production incomes accrued. Compensation of employees (wages and salaries) is the factor payment to labor. Nonlabor income—broken down in table 24

TABLE 24
Percentage Distribution of National Income by Type of Income, 1929–69

Year	Compensation of Employees	Proprietor's Income	Rental Income of Persons	Corporate Profits and IVA.*	Net Interest	Total National Income
1929	58.9	17.4	6.3	12.1	5.4	100.0
1940	64.2	16.1	3.6	12.1	4.0	100.0
1950	64.1	15.5	3.9	15.6	.8	100.0
1955	67.8	12.6	4.2	14.2	1.2	100.0
1960	71.0	11.1	3.8	12.0	2.0	100.0
1965	70.3	10.0	3.3	13.3	3.2	100.0
1967	71.5	9.5	3.2	12.0	3.7	100.0
1969	73.3	8.7	2.9	11.1	4.0	100.0

Calculated from the following sources: *The National Income and Product Accounts of the United States, 1929–1965,* pp. 14, 15; *Survey of Current Business* (July 1970), p. 20.

*Corporate profits before taxes, plus or minus inventory valuation and adjustment (IVA).

into proprietors' income, rental income of persons, corporate profits, and net interest—went to the factor capital.

According to the data in table 24, labor's share in national product has risen during the last four decades. In 1929 it accounted for 58.9% and in 1969 for 73.3% of national product. This rise implies a decline in the capital share. What components of the capital share did, however, decline? From table 24 it can be seen that a strong decline occurred in the share of proprietors' income and the rental incomes of persons. Both types of income frequently accrue to small and medium-sized businesses and to persons with moderate amounts of capital. The combined shares of proprietors' income and rental income of persons accounted for 23.7% of national income in 1929, but combined shares decreased to 11.6% in 1969. The change reflects how difficult it is for smaller businesses in the United States to keep up with nation-wide income increases. With the passage of time many proprietors of small businesses (especially small and medium-sized farms) became employees. These shifts in the labor force cannot explain all of the changes in income shares, but they were important. The decrease in the relative shares of proprietors' income and rental income of persons almost exactly offsets the increase in the labor share as given by compensation of employees.

The combined shares of corporate profits and net interest, on the other hand, remained rather stable (17.5% in 1929 and 15.1% in 1969). A good deal of these incomes accrue to owners of larger amounts of capital.

It is important to keep these underlying structural changes in mind when it is pointed out that the labor share of income rose in the United States. That it rose is not in dispute, but there is evidence that it did so essentially at the expense of the share of independent proprietors' income and rental income of persons, not at that of corporate profits and interest income.

The functional income distribution in the U.S. economy is of great interest to economists. Its empirical determination presents many conceptual problems, however, and is difficult with presently available data. At this time, we still have to be content with rough approximations as shown in table 24.

The Personal Income Distribution

General Considerations

Factors of production are owned by individuals, and it is to them that incomes ultimately accrue. Some individuals receive incomes from the supply of only one factor of production, for instance, labor. Others may receive incomes from several such factors. Some individuals derive high incomes, others low ones.

As a result of the working of the market and other forces

in an economy, a particular personal income distribution comes into existence. It tells us what percentage of all persons and what percentage of total aggregate income belong to different income brackets. The personal income distribution mirrors a country's economic and social structure, and it is therefore of considerable interest. Data on these distributions are now available for a number of countries, including the United States. In order to understand what the data represent, it is useful to discuss briefly some conceptual problems.

The first problem that arises is the choice of the unit to which income accrues. One way to solve this would be to have a truly personal income distribution which accounts for each individual separately, but this would obviously not be a good choice. Most individuals live in families and households, and many economic decisions are made in these micro units. These units are more meaningful and have often been chosen in personal income distributions.[2] The individual living by himself is in these distributions either considered a "one-person household," or he is put into a special category of "unattached individuals." Depending on what micro units are chosen and how the total population is grouped, the personal income distributions will, of course, differ.

The second problem concerns the definition of income. Personal income distributions are supposed to reflect the "economic position" of individuals in different income brackets. "Economic position" depends, however, not only on money income received but also on other types of income. What income concept should therefore be used? A broader income concept could include retained earnings in corporations, capital gains, and part of the corporation income tax. Further, incomes received in kind may be included.[3] If there is agreement on what definition of income to use, the problem still remains to choose income before or after redistribution through taxes, transfer payments, and subsidies. Some students believe the "primary" distribution (before redistribution) is more meaningful; others argue that the "secondary" distribution (after redistribution) gives a truer picture of the economic positions of individuals. To determine the actual redistribution is rather difficult, however, as it involves the thorny problem of tax and expenditure incidence in an economy. In some personal income distribution studies, the "primary" distribution is therefore simply income before, and the "secondary" distribution income after, the imposition of personal income taxes.

Personal income distributions are by their nature macro-economic. They refer to the aggregate of individuals in different income brackets. Based on empirical observations, they are thus ex-post statements. But what causes an individual, family, or household to be in a particular income bracket? How can an observed personal income distribution be rationalized?

It was shown that the neoclassical economic theory offers, under certain conditions, an explanation of observed functional income distributions. Granted the assumptions of a competitive market, which possesses a particular type of aggregate production function, the theory can explain the pricing of the factors of production and the distribution of income among cooperating resources. It cannot, however, explain the personal income distribution. At the present time it is not known how the functional and personal income distribution can be theoretically linked. The studies of personal income distributions that have been made so far are largely descriptive. In them a number of factors are singled out for an explanation of personal income, but a cohesive theoretical structure has not yet emerged.

Differences in individual or family incomes are usually explained by two types of "circumstances," those over which only little or no influence can be exerted, and those which can be changed through individual choice.

Into the first group fall the innate mental and physical abilities of an individual, the environment in which he grows up (favorable or unfavorable to the development of innate abilities), the material assets which he inherits, the ethnological group to which he belongs (discriminated against or favored), the tax system under which he has to live, the services which he is obliged to perform for the government (e.g., military service and the consequences thereof), and laws restricting him in the exercise of a profession. All of these are nonmarket factors. They are the "givens" for an individual, stemming from the cultural, political, and sociological setting in which he grows up and lives.

The second group of circumstances influencing personal income comprises those which the individual can influence through choice and taste. In a market economy, he may choose a profession in which he can best use his abilities and earn the highest possible income. He may be willing to undertake potentially lucrative, but risky business ventures. Out of a given income, he may manage to save enough to accumulate capital, which in turn may enable him to earn even more. In addition, he may arrange his personal life (marriage, number of children, raising of children, etc.) in such a way that his economic well-being is enhanced and not interfered with. In all of this, the individual has the possibility of choice. It is up to him to make what he considers to be the best of a given situation.

The task of making optimal choices is difficult, however, even in the best of circumstances. Each such choice involves uncertainty regarding the future, and each choice is restricted by the "given" factors mentioned above. Certain choices can be made only at certain times in life, and there is probably an optimal sequence of steps in the development and growth of an individual's abilities. It is exceedingly difficult to obtain a good education unless that education is begun sufficiently early in life. The talents of an individual, no matter how gifted and able he is, may largely be wasted if he is forced to eke out a living instead of attending a school or university at the proper time. Without education and training, the knowledge and insight required for proper choices may be deficient. Thus the initial givens, and those factors over which the individual has full or at least some measure of control, are intertwined and interrelated in a dynamic system. Its complexity may be one of the reasons why economic theory has thus far been unable to provide a satisfactory explanation for personal income, and for that matter for personal income distribution.

Changes in Personal Income Distribution between 1929 and 1962

In this section we propose to describe the changes in the United States personal income distribution between 1929 and 1962. During this period the GNP in constant 1958 prices increased by approximately 260%.

Together with this growth went an increase in household incomes. Many households in lower income brackets shifted into medium ones.[4] In turn, many of those in medium income brackets attained higher ones. We have summarized these shifts in personal income distribution in tables 25 and 26. From these it can be seen that the bulk of all households (67.2%) had incomes below $3,000 in 1929. By 1950 only 39.8% belonged to this bracket.

The upward shift continued during the next decade. The data for 1962 in table 26 are not strictly comparable with those in table 25, because of different constant prices, yet they indicate clearly the further development. Only 23.9% of all households still had less than $3,000 annual income in 1962. In the same year 28.3% of all households already had incomes over $7,500; and at the top, 15.3% had incomes over $10,000. More households earned more income, in nominal as well as in real terms.

But what were the relative changes in the income distribution between 1929 and 1962? Did the pre-income tax personal income distribution become more equal? To answer this question we have drawn in figure 7 two Lorenz curves for the years 1929 and 1962. The diagram has on its horizontal axis the cumulative percentage distribution of the number

TABLE 25

Percentage Distributions of Number of Families and
Unattached Individuals, and Aggregate Personal Income,
by Income Levels, 1929–50
(Income Before Income Taxes in 1950 Constant Prices)

Income Bracket: Dollars	1929		1941		1950	
	Numbers[1] %	Income[2] %	Numbers[1] %	Income[2] %	Numbers[1] %	Income[2] %
Under 1,000	15.9	2.0	15.1	2.7	7.9	.9
1,000 to 1,999	25.6	11.4	19.9	8.2	15.3	5.2
2,000 to 2,999	25.7	19.0	18.5	12.6	16.6	9.3
3,000 to 3,999	12.2	12.5	15.7	14.9	17.6	13.8
4,000 to 4,999	7.2	9.5	12.3	14.9	14.4	14.5
5,000 to 7,499	7.4	13.1	12.0	19.6	17.5	23.6
7,500 to 9,999	3.1	8.0	3.1	7.2	5.6	10.8
10,000 and over	2.9	24.5	3.4	19.9	5.1	21.9
Addendum: Total Number (Millions)	36.10		41.37		48.89	
Total Income (Bill. of Dollars)		121.39		151.59		217.26
Average Income, all brackets (Dollars)		3,363		3,664		4,444

Source: Historical Statistics of the United States, Colonial Times to 1957,
Series G.57–74, p. 165.

[1]Families and unattached individuals.
[2]Family Personal Income before income taxes.

of households. On its vertical axis it has the cumulative percentage distribution of incomes received. The diagonal line
AB indicates a perfectly equal distribution of income. The
more the points on the curve AB of the actually observed
distribution of income approach the diagonal, the greater the
equality of income distribution. In our diagram all points on
the 1962 Lorenz curve lie to the left of the 1929 curve. Since
there is no crossover of the two curves, the situation is unam-
biguous. The pretax household income distribution did become more equal between 1929 and 1962.[5] Income concentration diminished.

It is not known precisely what caused this change in
income distribution. Some students have stressed as a causa-

TABLE 26
Percentage Distributions of Number of Families and
Unattached Individuals, and Aggregate Personal Income,
by Income Levels, 1956–62
(Income Before Income Taxes in 1956 Constant Prices)

| Income Bracket | 1956 | | 1962 | |
| (Dollars) | Numbers[1] | Income[2] | Numbers[1] | Income[2] |
	%	%	%	%
Under 1,000	} 15.0	} 2.9	} 13.9	} 2.4
1,000 to 1,999				
2,000 to 2,999	10.6	4.5	10.0	3.9
3,000 to 3,999	13.2	7.9	11.2	6.0
4,000 to 4,999	14.2	10.9	11.5	8.0
5,000 to 7,499	25.1	26.1	25.1	23.8
7,500 to 9,999	11.0	16.0	13.0	17.2
10,000 and over	10.9	31.7	15.3	38.7
Addendum:				
Total Number (Millions)	52.8		57.9	
Total Income (Billions of Dollars)		310.9		375.7
Average Income all Brackets (Dollars)		5,888		6,489

Source: Historical Statistics of the United States: Continuation to 1962 and
Revisions (Washington, D.C., 1965), Series G57a to G74a, p. 23.

[1]Families and unattached individuals.
[2]Family Personal Income before Income Taxes

tive factor better educational opportunities, which accounted
for human capital formation and facilitated the access to bet-
ter-paying occupations. Another reason was perhaps a greater
interregional mobility of labor in response to better economic
opportunities. A third explanatory factor may have been the
slowly improving occupational opportunities for Negro and
other nonwhite families. It could thus be argued that, through
the removal or diminuition of institutional and other obsta-
cles, the efficiency of productive factors—in particular, low-
qualified labor—increased, and higher incomes could be
earned. The forces of the market economy would thus have
to be credited with achieving greater income equality. Yet
important nonmarket forces also had a considerable influence
on the pre-income tax personal income distribution during
this period. The country saw the emergence of a large system

LORENZ CURVES FOR UNITED STATES
PRE-INCOME TAX HOUSEHOLD INCOME
DISTRIBUTIONS IN 1929 AND 1962.

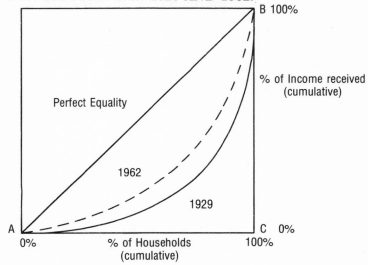

Fig. 7. Computed from tables 25 and 26.

of transfer payments. A social security system was created in
1935. Unemployment insurance, old-age pensions, and disability insurance mitigated the hardships of those who could
not work by maintaining their incomes in times of economic
distress. Also, public aid was given to the needy. Nonmarket
transfer payments became especially important for the lower
income brackets. Their incomes were increased. For the medium and upper income brackets, nonmarket factors also
influenced incomes, albeit in the other way. These groups
carried the burden of income transfers.

Our discussion has been restricted to the income distribution before income taxes and income transfers. We
pointed out earlier that considerable methodological problems arise if the income distribution after taxes and after
transfer payments is to be determined, problems with which
we cannot deal within the scope of this book. It may suffice
to indicate that the tax structure has tended to reduce income

inequality in the United States. It is generally believed that the country's tax structure is progressive: the higher the income, the more taxes are to be paid. Some students have pointed out, however, that the progressivity of the tax structure is only mild and that its redistributive effect is therefore limited. Economists usually say that it is not so much the revenue side but the expenditure side of government budgets that has the larger redistributive effect. Lower income brackets benefit more from public expenditures than higher ones do. The increases in government expenditures thus promoted income equality during the period under consideration.

Characteristics of the Personal Income Distribution in 1970

During the 1960s the U.S. economy experienced a vigorous expansion. Between 1962 and 1969 the GNP (in 1958 constant prices) increased from $529.8 billion to $727.1 billion. In 1970 growth temporarily ceased, and the figure stood at $724.1 billion. Average household income rose from $6,489 in 1962 to $10,001 in 1970. Part of this increase was admittedly due to inflation, but the real increases were substantial. The income increases generated further upward shifts in the personal income distribution. According to Department of Commerce data on money incomes of households, only 15.8% of all households had less than $3,000 income in 1970. On the other hand, 54.7% of all households had incomes over $8,000 and 19.1% received incomes over $15,000. At the top, 4% of all households obtained incomes over $25,000 (see table 27).

Many American households experienced an income breakthrough in the 1960s, and the overall picture was gratifying. Yet not everybody participated equally in the income growth. The rapid growth seems to have left some groups relatively behind, and there was dissatisfaction and dissent. As a consequence, efforts were made to bring into sharper

TABLE 27
Number of Households and Percentage Distribution of
Number of Households by Money Income in 1970
(Income before Income Taxes in 1970 Current Prices)

Income Bracket (Dollars)	Households Number (In Millions)	Percent
Under 1,000	1.934	3.0
1,000 to 1,999	4.296	6.7
2,000 to 2,999	3.944	6.1
3,000 to 3,999	3.799	5.9
4,000 to 4,999	3.656	5.7
5,000 to 5,999	3.814	5.9
6,000 to 6,999	3.811	5.9
7,000 to 7,999	3.928	6.1
8,000 to 9,999	7.966	12.4
10,000 to 14,999	14.938	23.2
15,000 to 24,999	9.715	15.1
25,000 to 49,999	2.252	3.5
50,000 and over	.322	.5
Totals	64.374	100.0

Addendum:
Median Household Income $8,734
Average Household Income $10,001

Source: U.S. Department of Commerce, *Current Population Reports,* Consumer Income Series P-60, no. 79 (July 27, 1971) pp. 1, 12.

focus particular structural features of the household income distribution. The age, education, residence, sex, and race of income recipients and the influence of such elements on money income were closely investigated. Some of these characteristics, such as age and education, have always been cited as explanatory factors for differences in personal income generated by a market economy that works along efficiency lines. Other characteristics, everything else being the same, should not make a great difference. If they do, then other than market forces must be involved in the determination of money incomes, and the problem of discrimination and use and abuse of economic power arises. We shall consider each characteristic separately.

An important relationship exists between the age of the head of household, who supposedly earns most if not all of the

TABLE 28

Age of Head of Household and Money Income in 1970
Percentage Distribution by Money Income Brackets

| Income Bracket (Dollars) | Age Brackets | | | | | |
	14–24	25–34	35–44	45–54	55–64	65 and over
0– 2,999	16.2	6.4	5.4	6.8	14.6	43.8
3,000– 4,999	17.8	8.2	6.9	7.7	11.2	21.0
5,000– 9,999	43.1	37.8	29.7	27.0	30.9	22.0
10,000–14,999	18.9	31.4	31.0	26.7	21.9	7.4
15,000–24,999	3.4	13.9	21.7	24.4	16.4	4.2
25,000–49,999	.3	1.8	4.8	6.5	4.4	1.4
50,000 and over	.1	.2	.5	.8	.8	.2
Total:	100.0	100.0	100.0	100.0	100.0	100.0
Addendum: Total of all Households, in 1000	4,707	11,847	11,739	12,509	10,952	12,622
% of Households in each age bracket, all household equal to 100.00	7.3	18.4	18.2	19.4	17.0	19.6
Average Money Income in Dollars	7,115	10,313	12,193	12,858	10,573	5,418
Median Money Income in Dollars	6,669	9,690	11,131	11,413	8,906	3,498

Source: Computed from *Current Population Reports,* Consumer Income Series P-60, no. 79 (July 27, 1971), p. 12. Because of rounding, details may not add up to total.

household income, and money income received. The data for 1970 show that in the United States the income at ages under 24 years is in the aggregate relatively low (see table 28). This can be explained by the need of young adults to get professionally established. Also, in cases of early marriages, wives may not be able to contribute to household incomes, especially if they must take care of small children. In the age bracket between 25 and 34 years the income increases. The highest household incomes are finally received between 45 and 54 years. In this age bracket many women take up work again because the children have grown up. The children themselves may contribute to household income. The U.S. household possesses its maximum earning power when its head is in the age bracket between 45 and 54 years. After this age a decline in income begins. In many cases children form their households and no longer contribute to the income of the parental household. Also, with advancing age, there is a higher incidence of disability and sickness. After the age of 65, there is still another decrease in average money income. This is the result of leaving the labor force, retirement, and a reliance on social security and pension funds for income. In 1970 more than 12.6 million households, or 19.6% of all households, belonged to the age group of 65 years and over. It was the largest single age group (see table 28).

One's lifetime income in the United States depends very much on the education one receives. A better education permits access to professions that require a higher skill and pay better. The data on educational attainment and household money incomes in 1970 revealed a significant relationship between education and income (see table 29). Heads of households with only an elementary school education remained very much in lower income brackets. Nearly half had annual incomes under $5,000. A completed high school education contributed substantially to the earning of higher incomes. A college education of 4 years or more further increased the earnings possibilities. Only 9.4% of all heads of households with a college education of 4 years or more had incomes below $5,000 in 1970, whereas 14.5% had incomes over $25,000.

The average household money incomes in 1970 speak for themselves—$5,747 earned by heads of households with less than eight years of elementary school, $10,422 by those with a complete four-year high school education, and $15,980 for those with four years or more of college.

Some other characteristics of the income distribution are shown in table 30. The United States has become an urbanized society, and the farm population is relatively

TABLE 29

Education and Money Income in 1970,
Percentage Distribution by Money Income Brackets,
Educational Attainment of Head of Household

Income Bracket (Dollars)	Elementary School		High School		College	
	Less than 8 Years	8 Years	1 to 3 Years	4 Years	1 to 3 Years	4 Years or more
0– 2,999	36.8	25.7	17.1	8.9	9.3	4.7
3,000– 4,999	19.5	17.1	13.6	9.1	7.9	4.7
5,000– 9,999	27.5	31.7	34.2	33.8	29.6	19.6
10,000–14,999	11.0	16.4	21.8	29.2	27.0	26.6
15,000–24,999	4.4	7.9	11.9	15.9	21.0	29.9
25,000–49,999	0.6	1.0	1.5	2.6	4.5	12.6
50,000 and over	.1	.1	.2	.2	.6	1.9
Total:	100.0	100.0	100.0	100.0	100.0	100.0
Addendum: Total of all Households (In 1000s)	9,027	8,255	10,583	20,142	7,602	8,765
% of Households by Educational Attainment of Head (All households equal 100.00)	14.0	12.8	16.4	31.3	11.8	13.6
Average Money Income (Dollars)	5,747	7,253	8,757	10,422	11,761	15,980
Median Money Income (Dollars)	4,290	5,987	7,833	9,708	10,506	13,947

Source: Computed from: *Current Population Reports,* Consumer Income, Series P-60, no. 79 (July 27, 1971), p. 12.

small. Households living in nonfarm residences had on the average a substantially higher money income ($10,108) than those living on farms ($7,519). More than 40% of households in farm residences had incomes under $5,000. For households in nonfarm residences the percentage was 26.7%. At the upper end of the income scale we find that 11.1% of all farm households had incomes over $15,000. For nonfarm households the percentage was 19.5%.

Of the 64.37 million households in 1970, 14.03 million had female heads of household. In the statistical class-

TABLE 30

Residence of Household, Sex of Head of Household, Race of Head of Household and Money Income in 1970 (Percentage Distribution by Money Income Brackets)

Income Bracket (Dollars)	Characteristics of Household					
	Residence		Sex		Race	
	Nonfarm	Farm	Male	Female	White	Negro
0– 2,999	15.4	24.1	8.5	41.9	14.5	28.2
3,000– 4,999	11.3	16.4	9.3	19.5	11.0	17.2
5,000– 9,999	30.3	32.4	31.4	26.2	30.2	31.9
10,000–14,999	23.6	15.8	27.3	8.5	24.1	14.6
15,000–24,999	15.4	9.3	18.4	3.3	16.0	7.3
25,000–49,999	3.6	1.7	4.3	.6	3.8	.8
50,000 and over	.5	.1	.6	.0[a]	.5	.1
Total:	100.0	100.0	100.0	100.0	100.0	100.0
Addendum: Total of all Households in 1000	61,723	2,651	50,338	14,036	57,575[b]	6,180[b]
% of all Households; All Households equal to 100.00 for each characteristic	95.9	4.1	78.2	21.8	89.4	9.6
Average Money Income, Dollars	10,108	7,519	11,368	5,100	10,351	6,761
Median Money Income, Dollars	8,849	6,269	10,097	3,745	9,096	5,538

Source: Computed from *Current Population Reports,* Consumer Income Series, P-60, no. 79 (July 27, 1971), p. 12.

[a]Less than one-half percent.
[b]Excluded are "Other Races," which accounted for 620,000 households. Incomes for these were not shown separately.

ification, female heads of household are female persons who are unmarried and living by themselves, divorced, or widowed. Often the female head of a household must care for children and is thus limited in her earning abilities. More than 61% of these types of households had annual money incomes under $5,000. The average for all households with a female head was only $5,100. In contrast, households with a male head had an average of $11,368.

Among the latter households, only 17.8% had incomes under $5,000.

Finally there is the much-discussed problem of race and money income. In table 30 we have given two distributions of households by money income brackets, one for white households, the other for Negro households. The third, small category "other races," consisting of 620,000 households, was omitted since no data were readily available for it.

According to the Department of Commerce data, 89.4% of all households were white, 9.6% Negro, and 1% belonged to other races in 1970. The average income was $10,351 for white households and $6,761 for Negro households. From table 30 it can be seen that the percentage of Negro households in lower income brackets is much higher than for white households. About 20.3% of all white households had incomes over $15,000, compared with only 8.2% for Negroes.

From the data presented one can infer the "favorable characteristics" for earning a high money income in the United States in 1970: being a white male between ages of 45 and 54 years, living in a nonfarm residence, and having four years or more of college education. Vice versa, the most "unfavorable characteristics" would be: being a female Negro of age 65 and over, living in a farm residence, having less than eight years of elementary school education. These were evidently the "circumstantial polar cases."

Regional Distribution of Income

The regional distribution of income is in most countries unequal. It is determined by the regional pattern of production, which in turn is the outcome of a number of interrelated factors, e.g., favorable production conditions, transport possibilities, and nearness to markets. In a market economy a particular spatial configuration of economic activity will develop in response to these factors. The United States is no exception to the rule of unequal patterns of regional production and income. Its geographic areas vary widely in their contributions to GNP, aggregate personal incomes, and per capita personal incomes.

For a study of the regional income distribution, a definition of "region" is necessary. From the economist's point of view it would be desirable to work with economic regions characterized by predominant economic attributes. However, the actual political subdivisions of a country often do not coincide with economic regions, and the available statistics may pertain to political regions only.

For the United States two sets of regional data are available. One pertains to the political subdivision by states, the other to groups of states which form nine large geographical regions. For want of better groupings, we shall use these data to show the present pattern of regional personal income distribution and changes therein during the period 1950 to 1970.

From table 31 it can be seen that aggregate personal income by states differs greatly. It ranged from $89.8 billion for the state of California to a mere $1.1 billion for the state of Wyoming in 1970. The income concentration by states was large: two states alone, California and New York, accounted for 22.3% of the nation's personal income. These two are the economic giants among the states. Five states accounted for 39.7%, ten states for 59.5%, and fifteen states for 70.4% of all personal income. At the top of the scale are eight heavily industrialized states, each with a personal income of over $30 billion. These are California, New York, Illinois, Pennsylvania, Ohio, Texas, Michigan, and New Jersey. At the bottom end, fifteen states have only 5.2% of all personal income. The five lowest-income states account for only 1.1% of all personal income.

Per capita personal incomes by states also show considerable differences. The average for all of the United States was $3,910 in 1970. Connecticut, the residence of many well-

TABLE 31

Aggregate Personal Income and Per Capita Personal Income by States in 1970 (Current Prices)

	Aggregate Personal Income			Per Capita
	Total (Billions of Dollars)	% of U.S. Personal Income	% Cumulative	Personal Income (Dollars)
California	89.8	11.3	11.3	4,469
New York	87.5	11.0	22.3	4,797
Illinois	50.3	6.3	28.6	4,516
Pennsylvania	46.0	5.8	34.4	3,893
Ohio	42.5	5.3	39.7	3,983
Texas	39.5	5.0	44.7	3,515
Michigan	36.0	4.5	49.2	4,043
New Jersey	32.7	4.1	53.3	4,539
Florida	24.6	3.1	56.5	3,584
Massachusetts	24.5	3.1	59.5	4,294
Indiana	19.7	2.5	62.0	3,773
Missouri	17.1	2.1	64.1	3,659
Maryland	16.8	2.1	66.2	4,247
Virginia	16.7	2.1	68.3	3,586
Wisconsin	16.5	2.1	70.4	3,722
North Carolina	16.2	2.0	72.4	3,188
Georgia	15.1	1.9	74.3	3,277
Connecticut	14.6	1.8	76.1	4,807
Minnesota	14.5	1.8	77.9	3,793
Washington	13.7	1.7	79.6	3,993
Tennessee	12.0	1.5	81.1	3,051
Louisiana	11.2	1.4	82.5	3,065
Iowa	10.5	1.3	83.8	3,714
Kentucky	9.9	1.2	85.0	3,060
Alabama	9.8	1.2	86.2	2,828
Kansas	8.6	1.1	87.3	3,804
Oklahoma	8.4	1.1	88.4	3,269
Colorado	8.3	1.1	89.4	3,751
Oregon	7.8	1.0	90.4	3,700
South Carolina	7.5	.9	91.3	2,908
Arizona	6.3	.8	92.1	3,542
Mississippi	5.7	.7	92.8	2,561
Nebraska	5.5	.7	93.5	3,700
Arkansas	5.3	.7	94.2	2,742
West Virginia	5.1	.6	94.8	2,929
Dist. of Columbia	4.2	.5	95.3	5,519
Rhode Island	3.7	.5	95.8	3,920

TABLE 31 (Continued)
Aggregate Personal Income and Per Capita Personal Income by States in 1970 (Current Prices)

| | Aggregate Personal Income | | | Per Capita |
	Total (Billions of Dollars)	% of U.S. Personal Income	% Cumulative	Personal Income (Dollars)
Utah	3.4	.4	96.2	3,210
Hawaii	3.4	.4	96.6	4,530
Maine	3.2	.4	97.0	3,243
New Mexico	3.1	.4	97.4	3,044
New Hampshire	2.7	.3	97.7	3,608
Nevada	2.3	.3	98.0	4,544
Montana	2.3	.3	98.3	3,381
Idaho	2.3	.3	98.6	3,206
Delaware	2.3	.3	98.9	4,233
South Dakota	2.1	.3	99.2	3,182
North Dakota	1.8	.2	99.4	2,937
Vermont	1.6	.2	99.6	3,491
Alaska	1.4	.2	99.8	4,676
Wyoming	1.1	.1	99.9	3,420
TOTAL	797.1	100.0		
Average for United States				3,910

Source: Statistical Abstract 1971, p. 314, table 497. Preliminary data for 1970: personal income is for this purpose defined as income received from all sources. For the sake of completeness the District of Columbia is included with the states. Because of rounding off, details may not add up to totals.

to-do people working in New York, had the highest per capita income, $4,807. Mississippi had the lowest, with $2,561. In seven states, per capita incomes were over $4,500, in five states they were between $4,499 and $4,000, in eighteen states between $3,999 and $3,500, and in fourteen states between $3,499 and $3,000. In six states incomes were below $3,000. There are thus rich and poor states, and the differences are sizable.

A somewhat different picture emerges when states are grouped into large regions. In this process smaller states are lumped together with larger ones and poorer with richer

TABLE 32

*Regional Distribution of Personal Income,
1950, 1960, and 1970
(Current Prices)*

Region	Aggregate Personal Income (in billions of dollars)			Per Capita Personal Income (in dollars)		
	1950	1960	1970	1950	1960	1970
New England	14.9	25.5	50.3	1,601	2,424	4,235
Middle Atlantic	53.0	88.2	166.2	1,751	2,574	4,461
East North Central	50.8	86.5	165.0	1,666	2,383	4,088
West North Central	20.1	31.9	60.1	1,428	2,066	3,677
South Atlantic	25.7	47.8	108.5	1,211	1,832	3,523
East South Central	10.5	17.8	37.4	915	1,476	2,908
West South Central	17.6	30.7	64.4	1,230	1,807	3,321
Mountain	7.2	14.5	29.1	1,418	2,094	3,507
Pacific	26.3	55.8	116.1	1,806	2,611	4,351
Total United States:	226.2	398.7	797.1	1,496	2,216	3,910

Source: Statistical Abstract 1971, p. 314, table 497. Personal income for this purpose is defined as income received from all sources during the calendar year by residents of each state.

ones. This provides a more balanced picture of overall regional performance in the United States. Table 32 presents data on aggregate personal income as well as per capita personal income for nine such regions. The data show that the Middle Atlantic region and the East North Central region had the highest aggregate personal incomes in 1970. The two regions cover a large part of the so-called "high income belt" in the United States, which extends roughly from the Atlantic coast at Boston westward to Milwaukee, then south to Chicago and back east to the Atlantic seashore at Baltimore. It covers much of the country's industrial heartland.

Next most important is the Pacific region, in which the state of California is economically preponderant, followed by the South Atlantic region. The income growth of both the Pacific and the South Atlantic regions was above the national average between 1950 and 1970. In the industrial, older, Middle Atlantic and East North Central regions the growth was below the national average.

Per capita personal income in the regions of the northeastern part of the country (New England, Middle Atlantic, and East North Central) and the Pacific region was above the national average of $3,910 in 1970. In all other regions it was below this figure. The East South Central region had the lowest per capita personal income, with $2,908.

8.
Property
Distribution

Volume and Composition of the Net Worth of Families in 1962

A household may either consume or save its income. If savings are made, capital formation occurs and there is an increase in wealth, which may take different forms. There may be increases in tangible assets, in liquid assets, or in claims against others. If the household income is high, everything else being the same, larger savings and a higher rate of capital formation are generally possible than with a lower income.

   With capital formation, more economic assets will be owned.[1] These have a net rate of return; they are earning assets and contribute to the incomes of those who own them. Property income is generated. Part or all of this may be saved and reinvested again. Thus, between income received and economic assets owned exist important interrelationships. If incomes are high, capital accumulation can be high; and once enough capital has been accumulated, incomes will be high. The process is a *dynamic* and *intertem-*

poral one. It is of great importance for a country's income and property distribution.

In investigating the actual property distribution in the United States, one must rely on scant official data and on a National Bureau of Economic Research study. The data limitations are serious. Our first data come from a survey of the financial characteristics of consumers conducted for the Board of Governors of the Federal Reserve System by the Census Bureau in 1963.[2] The second source is a report on personal wealth by the United States Treasury Department in 1962.[3] The third source is Lampman's study on top wealthholders in the United States.[4]

The Federal Reserve survey is based on field interviews from a sample of 3,600 families. It provides information on the total net worth of these families by income brackets and on the types of assets held by each income bracket in 1962. In an attempt to obtain as comprehensive as possible a picture of the net worth of American families, the income bracket range was greatly extended, the top bracket containing families with annual incomes of $100,000 and more. Table 33 presents the most important findings of this survey.

The average net worth (total assets held minus personal debt) rises with increasing incomes but at different rates. For family incomes below $3,000, the average net worth is $8,875. This net worth rises continuously, reaching $30,389 for the income bracket of $10,000 to $14,999. Above this, the net worth increases rapidly: $74,329 for the income bracket of $15,000 to $24,999, and $267,996 for the $25,000-to-$49,000 income bracket. The top income bracket, with $100,000 or more, had an average net worth of $1,554,152. The threshold for a more substantial increase in net wealth seems to have been $15,000 annual income in 1962.

Table 33 reveals another important feature. As the net worth increases, its composition changes. For those having incomes of up to $15,000, the largest single net worth item is the household's own house. For higher income brackets, investments, especially in stocks, gain in importance. Stocks

TABLE 33

Composition of Net Worth of American Households
(Families and Unattached Individuals) on 31 December 1962
(Average Net Worth and Assets Held in Dollars, 1962 Prices)

Income Bracket	Total Net Worth	Tangible Assets			Business & Professions	Life Ins.[3] Annuities Ret. Plans	Liquid Assets	Investment Assets				Misc. Assets	Pers.[4] Debt
		All	Own Home[1]	Auto.[2]				All	Stocks	Marketable Bonds	Others		
0– 2,999	8,875	3,901	3,752	149	1,418	190	1,330	2,128	1,480	201	448	113	205
3,000– 4,999	10,914	3,956	3,544	412	1,902	635	1,738	2,925	818	19	2,088	137	378
5,000– 7,499	15,112	5,615	4,973	643	2,050	1,135	1,716	3,710	2,365	18	1,326	1,339	453
7,500– 9,999	21,243	8,367	7,499	868	2,577	1,879	2,722	4,779	1,476	44	3,258	1,632	712
10,000–14,999	30,389	10,873	9,527	1,346	5,174	2,975	4,233	6,969	3,761	316	2,893	749	584
15,000–24,999	74,329	17,004	15,188	1,816	9,088	5,196	9,241	30,638	18,733	1,445	10,460	3,664	502
25,000–49,999	267,996	35,090	32,215	2,875	66,144	10,819	19,098	92,663	58,111	4,742	29,810	48,736	4,553
50,000–99,999	789,582	48,764	45,961	2,803	251,977	19,559	41,845	345,728	204,665	71,971	69,092	86,313	4,604
100,000 and over	1,554,152	89,645	85,634	4,011	288,915	32,309	54,426	1,004,246	758,253	121,985	124,008	96,879	12,268
Addendum: All Households	22,588	6,612	5,975	637	3,913	1,376	2,579	7,063	4,072	456	2,535	1,528	483

Source: "Survey of Financial Characteristics of Consumers." *Federal Reserve Bulletin* (March 1964), p. 293, supplementary table 2. For definition of various assets see p. 290 of this work. The table is reprinted as table 489 in *Statistical Abstract of the United States, 1967.*

[1] Less debt secured on homes.
[2] Less debt on automobiles.
[3] Cash surrender values of life insurances less loans. Amounts which could have withdrawn from retirement plans on December 31, 1962; amounts which would have been paid for annuities on December 31, 1962.
[4] Nonbusiness, personal debt, e.g., installment debt on consumer durables. Automobile debt excluded.

are followed by the net worth of business and professions. Thus, as incomes and net worths increase, the willingness to hold riskier, higher-yield assets also increases.[5]

A third feature involves the liquidity preference of the top wealth-holders. Liquid asset holdings in the form of checking and savings deposits, shares in savings and loan associations and credit unions, and U.S. savings bonds increase absolutely with larger net worth. However, beginning with the income bracket of $25,000 to $49,999, liquid assets as a percentage of total assets decrease sharply. The two lowest income brackets retained on the average more than 15% of all net worth in the form of liquid assets. For the highest bracket this figure is only 3.5%. Great wealth permits one to have relatively less liquid assets.

The asset structure shown in table 33 is in general accord with what economic theory predicts for the asset choice under risk of investors who face different asset constraints.[6] With higher incomes and more wealth, the risk aversion decreases.

The Distribution of the Nation's Wealth

The distribution of a nation's wealth between families (or households) is the result of a complicated, dynamic process involving both market and nonmarket forces. The social importance of the distribution is paramount. There are, however, no direct data on this aspect of American economic life. Such information as exists is obtained indirectly and consists of estimates which may involve large margins of error.

Under the federal estate tax law a return must be filed with the Internal Revenue Service for each decedent who had a gross estate above a prescribed minimum, $60,000 since 1942. Hence, returns must be filed for only a small fraction of all Americans dying each year. Those that are filed, however, provide valuable information on the top wealth holders in the country. Through a special method, known as the "estate-multiplier" method, it is possible to infer from these returns something about the total population of top wealth-holders. Furthermore, in conjunction with independent estimates of the nation's capital stock, an overall property distribution can be estimated. This is what Lampman did in his 1962 study for the National Bureau of Economic Research.

According to Lampman, the lower 50% of all "American spending units" received about 23% of all money income in 1953, but they owned only 4% of all net worth.[7] Eighty percent of all families earned about 54% of all money income and owned approximately 24% of all net worth. Ninety percent earned 69% of all money income and owned 43% of all net worth. Thus the upper 10% of all spending units received 31% of all income and owned 57% of all net worth. Lampman further estimated that the top 2% of all families held 29% of the nation's wealth in 1953. For later years no comparable figures are available.

In the history of economic analysis the hypothesis has been advanced, especially by Karl Marx and his followers, that capitalist market economies will experience an ever-increasing concentration of property in the hands of a few. There would be a polarization of the population into two groups, a large propertyless one, and a small one which would hold nearly all of the nation's wealth. This would result in dire consequences for the economy. A collapse of the system would ultimately be inevitable. Such a polarization has so far not occurred in the U.S. economy, and it is doubtful that it ever will.

Indeed Lampman's data on the wealth held by the top one percent of all adult wealth-holders in the period 1922–53 indicate the opposite. He found that this top share decreased. It was 32% in 1922, 38% in 1929, 22% in 1949, and 25% in 1953. The decline was attributed to relative changes in the price of assets, less savings by the top wealth group, and changing practices in the transfer of wealth. What has happened to this top wealth share after 1953 is unknown. Rising stock values over the last decade and a half may have worked against further declines.

The available data indicate that the property distribution in the United States is distinctly more unequal than the income distribution. There is a heavy concentration of property ownership, as is also the case in other market economies. It is difficult to obtain international data on property distributions. In one case, however, a comparison could be made between the United States in 1953 and England and Wales in 1946–47. Surprisingly, the property distribution in socialist-minded England was found to be even more unequal than that of the United States.[8]

Some Characteristics of the Top Wealth-holders in 1962

Who are the top wealth-holders in the United States? Little direct information is available, but the Treasury Department has published some estimates on the top wealth-holders, based on estate tax returns. The latest year for which these data are available is 1962.[9] It is estimated that there were in that year 4.132 million persons who possessed a gross estate of $60,000 or more. Of these, 61.4% were men and 38.6%, women. The majority of all male wealth-holders, 2.12 million, were married; 0.194 million were single and 0.159 million widowed. Of the female wealth-holders, 0.761 million were married, 0.188 million single, and 0.549 million widowed. For men, the most numerous wealth-holder age group was age 50 years and under, whereas for women it was the age group between 50 and 64 years. The latter age group no doubt included many widows who inherited their estates through their husbands' deaths.

The majority of all wealth-holders owned gross estates

worth less than $200,000. Those with less than $100,000 wealth numbered 1.593 million, those with $100,000 to $200,000, 1.627 million. In the next wealth bracket, $200,000 to $500,000, fell 692,000 persons. After that the numbers rapidly decreased. There were 71,000 millionaires, wealth-holders with gross estates over one million dollars each. At the very top, 2,000 persons had estates each worth over $10 million.

The aggregate asset holdings of the top wealth-holders were estimated at $752 billion. Of this, 43.3% consisted of corporate stock and 25% of real estate. The rest was held in the form of bonds (6.4%), cash (9.4%), notes and mortgages (4%), insurance equity (2.1%) and other assets (9.8%). To finance these asset holdings, the top group incurred a $82.7 billion debt, so that its net worth was $669.3 billion.

9.
Use of the
Nation's Product

Some General Observations

The ultimate purpose of all production is consumption. A large part of a nation's annual product is directly consumed by the population. It is used for food, shelter, clothing, transportation, and other necessities and amenities of life. The sum of the expenditures for these purposes is consumption proper, referred to as "personal consumption."

A second part of a nation's product is indirectly consumed. It is used for investment. Efficient production in developed economies occurs in a roundabout manner and requires time and a large man-made capital stock. In each production period, part of the capital stock gets worn out and must be replaced if productive capacity is to remain intact. Thus a certain fraction of the product must be devoted to reinvestment. If more is invested than that needed for reinvestment, the capital stock grows and productive capacity increases. In this case "net investment" occurs. Replacement investment plus net investment are conventionally referred to as "gross investment."

The third use of a nation's product is that of the government. Modern market economies are mixed economies. In these the government supplies, in accordance with collective preferences, certain types of goods and services such as national defense, courts of justice, police protection, and highways.

A fourth use of the nation's product is for exports. Most modern market economies are open economies. Because of comparative advantages in production, tastes of the population, and other factors, it is often advantageous for them to import certain goods and services from foreign countries. Imports are paid for with the export of domestically produced goods and services. If exports equal imports, the use of the national product equals its production.[1] If exports exceed imports, fewer goods and services are available at home than are produced. In this case the country uses part of its product to acquire claims against foreigners. If on the other hand more is imported than exported, more can be used at home than is produced. An excess of imports over exports either reduces the country's existing claims against foreigners, or it leads to negative claims (indebtedness). It is customary in national income accounting to consolidate exports and imports into "net exports," which are defined as the difference between total exports and total imports of goods and services. Net exports may be positive, zero, or negative.

The sum of all uses of a nation's product is referred to as "aggregate demand," the counterpart of "aggregate supply," or the gross product of a nation. In national income accounting, the aggregate demand is ex-post always equal to aggregate supply. This is a necessity within the conceptual framework of national income accounting: what is produced in any one period must somehow be used, whether these uses have been intended or unintended, whether they have been in line with expectations or have led to disappointments. This being the case, one cannot detect the underlying causes for a particular volume and structure of aggregate supply and demand from national income statistics alone. In particular, one cannot say whether aggregate demand or aggregate supply acted as an effective constraint on the economy.

A mixed market economy is a complex, interdependent, dynamic system. The theory is that consumers try to maximize consumption and producers try to maximize profits, both pursuits occurring in accord with private preferences. Public preferences act in conjunction with private ones. With given resources the two sets of preferences determine a particular volume and structure of production. Production in turn generates income. A particular income distribution emerges and, one stage further removed, a particular property distribution evolves. But who uses the product? What factors determine this use? There are many: present incomes, the income distribution, the existing volume of economic assets and their distribution (property distribution), relative prices, and the expectations as to future changes in all of these combine to determine the use of the nation's product. At the same time, the ways in which the product is used, or is expected to be used, have an influence on production. Production and uses are interconnected and interdependent. Efforts to concentrate through aggregate economic analysis on just one alone are not satisfactory, to wit: the neoclassical preoccupation with aggregate supply and the Keynesian stress on aggregate demand.

In a mixed market economy a variety of real and financial variables simultaneously interact. Some of these reflect resource constraints and technologies and belong to the domains of the natural sciences and engineering. In the analysis of these variables a certain mechanistic mathematical approach is justified. Other variables are, however, of a sociological or psychological nature and reflect the experiences, hopes, aspirations, and expectations of the human beings in the economic process. To treat these variables in a mechanistic way would be to ingore their very essence. Naive statistical methods in the field of macro-economics may do more harm than good, through averaging, careless aggregation, and treating entities as homogeneous when they are not. They

TABLE 34
Use of Gross National Product, 1929–70
(Billion Dollars, Current Prices)

| | Total Gross National Product | Personal Consumption Expenditures | Gross Private Domestic Investment | Net Exports, Goods and Services | Government Purchases of Goods & Services | | | | |
| | | | | | Total | Federal Government | | | State and Local |
						Total	National Defense	Other	
1929	103.1	77.2	16.2	1.1	8.5	1.3	1.3		7.2
1930	90.4	69.9	10.3	1.0	9.2	1.4	1.4		7.8
1931	75.8	60.5	5.6	.5	9.2	1.5	1.5		7.7
1932	58.0	48.6	1.0	.4	8.1	1.5	1.5		6.6
1933	55.6	45.8	1.4	.4	8.0	2.0	2.0		6.0
1934	65.1	51.3	3.3	.6	9.8	3.0	3.0		6.8
1935	72.2	55.7	6.4	.1	10.0	2.9	2.9		7.1
1936	82.5	61.9	8.5	.1	12.0	4.9	4.9		7.0
1937	90.4	66.5	11.8	.3	11.9	4.7	4.7		7.2
1938	84.7	63.9	6.5	1.3	13.0	5.4	5.4		7.6
1939	90.5	66.8	9.3	1.1	13.3	5.1	1.2	3.9	8.2
1940	99.7	70.8	13.1	1.7	14.0	6.0	2.2	3.8	8.0
1941	124.5	80.6	17.9	1.3	24.8	16.9	13.8	3.1	7.9
1942	157.9	88.5	9.8	.0	59.6	51.9	49.4	2.5	7.7
1943	191.6	99.3	5.7	-2.0	88.6	81.1	79.7	1.4	7.4
1944	210.1	108.3	7.1	-1.8	96.5	89.0	87.4	1.6	7.5
1945	211.9	119.7	10.6	-.6	82.3	74.2	73.5	.7	8.1
1946	208.5	143.4	30.6	7.5	27.0	17.2	14.7	2.5	9.8
1947	231.3	160.7	34.0	11.5	25.1	12.5	9.1	3.5	12.6
1948	257.6	173.6	46.0	6.4	31.6	16.5	10.7	5.8	15.0
1949	256.5	176.8	35.7	6.1	37.8	20.1	13.3	6.8	17.7

Year									
1950	284.8	191.0	54.1	1.8	37.9	18.4	14.1	4.3	19.5
1951	328.4	206.3	59.3	3.7	59.1	37.7	33.6	4.1	21.5
1952	345.5	216.7	51.9	2.2	74.7	51.8	45.9	5.9	22.9
1953	364.6	230.0	52.6	.4	81.6	57.0	48.7	8.4	24.6
1954	364.8	236.5	51.7	1.8	74.8	47.4	41.2	6.2	27.4
1955	398.0	254.4	67.4	2.0	74.2	44.1	38.6	5.5	30.1
1956	419.2	266.7	70.0	4.0	78.6	45.6	40.3	5.3	33.0
1957	441.1	281.4	67.8	5.7	86.1	49.5	44.2	5.3	36.6
1958	447.3	290.1	60.9	2.2	94.2	53.6	45.9	7.7	40.6
1959	483.7	311.2	75.3	.1	97.0	53.7	46.0	7.6	43.3
1960	503.7	325.2	74.8	4.0	99.6	53.5	44.9	8.6	46.1
1961	520.1	335.2	71.7	5.6	107.6	57.4	47.8	9.6	50.2
1962	560.3	355.1	83.0	5.1	117.1	63.4	51.6	11.8	53.7
1963	590.5	375.0	87.1	5.9	122.5	64.2	50.8	13.5	58.2
1964	632.4	401.2	94.0	8.5	128.7	65.2	50.0	15.2	63.5
1965	684.9	432.8	108.1	6.9	137.0	66.9	50.1	16.8	70.1
1966	747.6	465.5	120.8	5.1	156.2	77.4	60.6	16.8	78.8
1967	793.9	492.1	116.6	5.2	180.1	90.7	72.4	18.3	89.4
1968	865.0	535.8	126.5	2.5	200.2	99.5	78.0	21.5	100.7
1969	931.4	577.5	139.8	1.9	212.2	101.3	78.8	22.5	110.8
1970	976.5	616.7	135.7	3.6	220.5	99.7	76.6	23.1	120.9

Sources: For the years 1929 to 1966: *Economic Report of the President*, p. 227, table B-1; for the years 1967 to 1970: *Statistical Abstract 1971*, p. 305, table 484.

may conceal rather than reveal the true relationships. The danger is what the Germans call a "mechanistische Verödung," which means a mechanistic approach without judgmental content.

During the last two decades, 1950–70, much work has been done on aggregate supply and demand, and many macro-economic models have been set up, some simplistic, some sophisticated and elaborate.[2] With the aid of these models, economists hoped to improve their understanding of the working of a dynamic mixed market system. Their ultimate aim, to develop models that could be helpful for economic policy decision making, was an ambitious one. Such models had to be realistic, but they could not be better than the economic theories on which they were based. For many of the observed economic phenomena, e.g. inflation cum unemployment, no satisfactory theory as yet exists. As things stand, many theoretical and conceptual problems must still be overcome before macro-economic models can be built that can satisfactorily explain and predict aggregate supply and demand.

Uses of the U.S. GNP between 1929 and 1970

In the use of the U.S. GNP during the last four decades, two periods can be distinguished. The first, from 1929 to 1949, spans the Great Depression, World War II, and the immediate postwar years. During this time the economy experienced large swings in economic activity. Associated with these swings were substantial changes in the use of the nation's product. The second period ranged from 1950 to 1970; it was characterized by a high degree of economic stability and a fairly stable pattern in the use of GNP (table 34).

The year 1929 was for the American economy a truly remarkable one. In it, a seven-year-long investment boom climaxed, and increases in industrial production and GNP were large. According to Kuznets's data, gross capital formation (in 1929 prices) increased by $3.3 billion and GNP by $6.5 billion.[3] It was the peak year of the twenties and simultaneously the beginning of the worst depression in modern history.

Whether the downturn could have been avoided is a moot question. There has never been a consensus on the reasons for this downturn, though important factors contributing to the calamity have been singled out: overinvestment in particular industries, creation of excess capacity, speculative optimism in view of rapid technological progress, financial excesses, questionable bank policies and a worsening international situation, with balance-of-payments difficulties. Some economists believe that a government with today's policy tools at its disposal could have moderated or even avoided the disaster. In any case, the year 1929 still had the full forward thrust of the economy. Its product use is therefore of special interest: 74.8% ($77.2 billion) of the GNP went for consumption, 15.7% ($16.2 billion) for gross private investment, 8.2% ($8.5 billion) for government use, and 1.1% ($1.1 billion) for net exports.

With the onset of the Great Depression, private investment expenditures fell rapidly. By 1932 they had decreased to only one billion dollars, or 1.7% of GNP. Personal consumption expenditures dwindled, to $48.6 billion. On the other hand, government purchases of goods and services did not decline too much. They amounted to $8.5 billion in 1929 and $8.1 billion in 1932. Their relative share was 13.9% of GNP in 1932. Adverse short-run as well as long-run expectations had caused private investment to contract sharply. It proved to be the most volatile and unstable element of aggregate demand. With the return of some confidence later in the 1930s, the situation improved and more investment was forthcoming, but at an agonizingly slow speed. In 1939, when real GNP had finally reached the 1929 level again, the product use had also more or less returned to the old pattern: 73.8% consumption, 10.2% gross private investment, 14.7% government purchases of goods and services, and 1.2% net exports.

World War II brought on new and drastic changes. The U.S. economy became a war economy. Productive resources were fully used, and the GNP in 1958 constant prices increased from $227.2 billion in 1940 to $355.2 billion in 1945. The war necessitated huge purchases of goods and services by the government; private consumption and investment had to be restrained. In 1944 private consumption expenditures accounted for only 51.5% of GNP, a record low. Investment was down to 3.4%, and net exports to −0.9%. Government expenditures on the other hand were up to 46% of GNP. There was much redirecting in the uses of the nation's product.

The end of hostilities in 1945 caused a rapid decrease in government expenditures. Though some economists questioned what could take their place to keep up aggregate demand and prevent the spectre of another recession, or even depression, the war had caused a hugh backlog in unsatisfied consumer and investment demand. Also, there were growing exports, partly because of aid programs. These factors combined proved to be enough to propel the economy so that it was possible to maintain high levels of production. In 1949, consumption expenditures accounted again for 68.9% of GNP, private investment for 13.9%, government expenditures for 14.8% and net exports for 2.4%.

The years 1950 and 1951 then saw two sharp investment spurts, but the economic consequences of another event soon overshadowed everything else. The Korean war broke out, dashing all hopes of an early normalization of international relations. Government purchases of goods and services, notably for military use, rose to a new high level and stayed there, ranging between 18% and 23.1% of GNP between 1951 and 1970.

Beginning with 1951 we can observe the emergence of a rather stable expenditure pattern in the U.S. economy. Between 61.9% and 64.8% of the GNP was annually spent on consumption. Investment expenditures, hitherto rather volatile, became much more stable and varied only between 13.6% and 16.1%, except in 1951, when the percentage was

18.1%. Also, government expenditures reached a new high level, accounting in most years for over 20% of GNP. The greater stability in investment expenditures and a relative increase in government expenditures were significant economic features of the period after 1950. This was partly because of economic policy efforts to prevent undesirable gyrations in economic activity and to achieve economic growth, and partly the consequence of the country's adaptation to the new postwar international situation.

The new and more stable use of GNP reflected important changes on the domestic as well as the international scene. With respect to private investment there was in the business community a new high degree of confidence that major depressions (though perhaps not shorter recessions) could be prevented through appropriate economic policy measures. As far as government expenditures were concerned, they were high. Chances of their decrease were remote; on the contrary, there were considerable domestic pressures to increase them further. Especially there was a quest for larger programs in the area of health, welfare, and education to help the society's less privileged groups. Furthermore, international developments were such that defense expenditures could not be decreased sharply without jeopardizing national security. Once the country became involved in the Vietnam war, defense outlays had to be further increased. These war-related expenditures were so large that they led to budgetary troubles and strong inflationary pressures.

The federal government's budget had become large. Changes in it for policy purposes, in conjunction with appropriate monetary policy measures, were expected to have enough leverage to keep the economy on an even keel. In reality this proved to be a difficult task.

Beyond the major changes in expenditures outlined above, there were during the past four decades many smaller ones associated with shorter swings in economic activity. These are described in the specialized literature on business cycles.

TABLE 35

Use of Gross National Product—Expenditures by Type of Product, Selected Years, 1929–70
(Percentage Distribution)

	1929	1940	1950	1960	1970
Goods Output	54.4	56.2	57.0	51.5	48.6
Services	34.5	35.5	30.5	37.2	41.9
Structures	11.1	8.3	12.4	11.3	9.5
Total Expenditures	100.0	100.0	100.0	100.0	100.0
Addendum: Total Expenditures in Bill. Dollars, Current Prices	103.1	99.7	284.8	503.7	976.5

Source: Calculated from *Statistical Abstract, 1971,* "Gross National Product in Current Prices," p. 305, table 484.

We have so far been concerned with the large expenditure categories—consumption, investment, exports, and public uses—but there is another aspect of the use of GNP we may briefly discuss. This is the use by type of product. It has been argued that in an advanced industrialized economy there is, over time, an increase in the demand for services relative to that for goods. The reasons for this are partly technological, partly psychological and sociological, manyfold, and complex. Table 35, which shows the available data for the United States, confirms a strong increase in the demand for services relative to that of goods. In 1929, 54.4% of all outlays were made for goods, 34.5% for services, and 11.1% for structures. In 1970, 48.6% was spent on goods, 41.9% on services, and 9.5% on structures. Similar changes in aggregate demand have been observed in other developed countries.

Personal Consumption Expenditures

During the last twenty-five years, about two-thirds of total aggregate demand consisted of personal consumption expenditures. Because this is such a large share, fluctuations in consumer expenditures can greatly affect economic stability. To counter such fluctuations through appropriate economic policy measures, it is necessary to understand what determines personal consumption in a contemporary market economy. After World War II, much research was devoted to this problem in the United States.[4]

The traditional neoclassical economic theory posits that the consumer is a utility maximizer. He is confronted with a given set of prices for factors of production and products and derives a certain income in the market from the use of the factors of production that he owns. As he makes his consumption decisions, he takes into consideration not only present but also future consumption. It is possible that he will first determine the amount of current consumption. Subsequently, he may determine the composition of his present consumption. In most cases, however, decisions on the volume and composition of present consumption are interrelated, and they are made simultaneously.

The sum of all individual consumption expenditures constitutes the aggregate "personal consumption expenditures." To estimate and predict these expenditures requires an intimate knowledge of the working of the market system, what income consumers will obtain, what consumer preferences are, and how consumers would react to changes in prices, and so on. To handle this problem adequately, much detailed information is necessary.

Neoclassical theory of personal consumption dovetails perfectly with models of a competitive market economy characterized by price and wage flexibility, but once the relevance of these models to the actual working of contemporary market economies was questioned, neoclassical consumption theory also came under attack. New theoretical explanations were given.

In 1935 John Maynard Keynes provided a theoretical model of income determination, an integral part of which is the consumption function. The all-important feature of this function is the income constraint on personal consumption.

Keynes held that consumers will consume a fairly stable share of their income and that they possess a "propensity to consume." About the latter he wrote: "The fundamental psychological law, upon which we are entitled to depend with great confidence both a priori from our knowledge of human nature and from the detailed facts of experience, is that men are disposed, as a rule and on the average, to increase their consumption as income increases, but not by as much as the increases in their income."[5] Thus developed the analytical concepts of an average and marginal "propensity to consume." From the "marginal propensity to consume" the multiplier was derived which in turn permitted the determination of the income increases caused by autonomous private investment expenditures or government expenditures. Some economists believed that the consumption function was Keynes's greatest theoretical contribution.

The "propensity to consume" became the crucial link between investment and consumption, replacing a host of other, more subtle, variables that, according to neoclassical theory, explained consumer choices and expenditures. Particularly, the role of the price system in the determination of consumer choices was played down, if not completely ignored. The novelty was that savings were no longer considered to be influenced by the rate of interest and the structure and volume of assets connected with it. On the other hand, Keynes did stress the importance of the rate of interest for investment choices. In his model there coexist thus an interest-insensitive consumer sector and an interest-sensitive investment sector. This feature makes one wonder whether Keynes may have had in mind two decision-making groups in the economy, one possessing the bulk of all assets and being interest-sensitive, the other without any large assets and therefore interest-insensitive. Such a theoretical dichotomy may have its merits for some economies but it is not very useful for that of the United States.

The income constraint on consumption is an enabling condition or feasibility condition. It is conceivable that the

former can be all-important in an economy in which income
is so low that all, or nearly all, of it must be used to meet
subsistence consumption. The income constraint becomes in
this case binding. The contemporary U.S. economy is not of
this type. The country has a large middle and upper-middle
income group. People in these groups make most of the consumer decisions, and their spending accounts for the bulk of
all consumer expenditures. They hold real and liquid assets
and they have ready access to consumer credit. Their consumption pattern includes not only perishable goods which
must be currently bought, but also durable goods which are
much more in the nature of investments, since they yield
services over several years and their acquisition can often be
postponed for a considerable time if necessary. Further, this
large section of the population is, through modern news me-
dia, generally well informed about political and economic
developments. The formation of consumer expectations is facilitated and leads to a uniformity in attitudes that in turn
tends to reduce the random element in buying. The American consumer can choose; he has leeway in his purchases. It
is important to know not only that he *can* buy with his income but *what, when,* and *how much* he will buy.

A host of factors influences consumer expenditures—
present and past incomes, previous peak consumption, prices,
interest rates, assets held, age, and family structure, as well as
expectations the consumer forms. After studying the Keynesian consumption function and understanding its shortcomings, economists soon began to experiment with more elaborate functions incorporating other variables besides income.
There is now a large body of writing on consumption functions (see, for instance, the works listed at the end of this
chapter). Generally, a partial return to the neoclassical approach to consumption and income occurred, giving more
weight to consumer choices and the factors underlying them.

In the United States, aggregate personal consumption
expenditures in current prices have risen substantially between 1929 and 1970. In 1929 these amounted to $77.2 billion,

TABLE 36

Aggregate Personal Consumption Expenditures by Type of Product, Selected Years, 1929–69

	1929	1940	1950	1960	1969
Food, Beverages and Tobacco[1]	27.0	31.0	30.4	26.9	22.8
Clothing, Accessories and Jewelry	14.2	12.4	12.4	10.2	10.3
Personal Care	1.4	1.4	1.3	1.6	1.7
Housing[2]	14.2	12.7	11.1	14.2	14.5
Household Operations[3]	13.6	14.6	15.4	14.4	14.1
Medical Care Exp.	4.5	4.9	4.6	5.9	7.4
Personal Business	6.5	5.1	3.6	4.6	5.5
Transportation[4]	9.7	10.0	12.9	13.3	13.5
Recreation	5.5	5.2	5.8	5.6	6.3
Other[5]	3.4	2.6	2.4	3.3	3.8
Total Expenditures	100.0	100.0	100.0	100.0	100.0
Addendum: Total Expenditures in Bill. Dollars Current Prices	77.2	70.8	191.0	325.2	577.5

Source: For 1950, 1960 and 1969, *Statistical Abstract 1971*, p. 308, table 490. For 1929 and 1940, calculated from data in *Historical Statistics of the United States,* p. 178, table G191–218. The total expenditures for 1929 are given there as $78.9 billion, for 1940 as $71.8 billion.

[1]Includes alcoholic beverages.
[2]Rental value of houses and apartments. Actual or imputed rent.
[3]Includes furniture, equipment, electricity, gas, water, fuels, telephone, domestic services, and others.
[4]Own and purchased transportation.
[5]Includes expenditures for private education, research, religious and welfare activities, foreign travel and others.

but they reached $616.7 billion in 1970. Yet it is not only the increase in total volume but also the changes in the structure of these expenditures that are of interest.

In official statistics, consumer expenditures are conveniently broken down into large groups; thus intertemporal shifts can be traced. The largest part of all consumer expenditures is traditionally for commodities of the "food, beverages, and tobacco products" group. In 1929 these accounted for 27% of all expenditures. By 1969 the share was down to 22.8% (see table 36). A similar decrease can be observed for the "clothing, accessories, and jewelry" category. Whereas 14.2% of all

TABLE 37

Consumption Expenditures of Families
in Different Income Brackets in 1960
(Current Prices, Percentage Distribution)

	Income Brackets (Dollar Income after Taxes)								
	Under 1000	1000 to 2000	2000 to 3000	3000 to 4000	4000 to 5000	5000 to 6000	6000 to 7500	7500 to 10,000	10,000 and over
Food	25.6	31.0	29.3	26.7	25.8	25.4	24.4	24.1	21.3
Alcoholic Beverages	1.2	1.1	1.1	1.3	1.4	1.5	1.6	1.7	1.9
Tobacco	2.1	2.4	2.2	2.2	2.1	2.0	1.9	1.7	1.2
Housing*	32.7	33.9	33.4	30.6	29.8	29.6	29.0	27.6	27.7
Clothing	6.1	6.4	7.8	8.9	9.6	9.9	10.4	11.2	12.0
Automobile Transportation	3.8	4.6	6.8	11.6	13.6	13.9	13.9	14.5	13.2
Other Transportation	3.3	1.8	1.7	1.6	1.4	1.2	1.4	1.5	2.4
Medical Care	10.3	8.4	8.5	7.6	6.5	6.5	6.6	6.4	6.2
Personal Care	3.3	3.1	3.3	3.1	3.0	3.0	2.9	2.9	2.6
Recreation	3.2	2.1	2.6	3.3	3.5	3.7	4.1	4.5	4.3
Reading	1.0	.9	.9	.8	.9	.9	.9	.9	.9
Education	1.2	.5	.5	.6	.6	.8	1.0	1.1	2.3
Miscellaneous	6.3	3.8	1.9	1.6	1.7	1.6	2.0	2.0	3.4
Total	100.0	100.0	100.0	100.0	100.0	100.0	100.0	100.0	100.0
Addendum:									
Average Consumption Expenditures in Dollars	2,389	2,038	2,840	3,884	4,624	5,288	6,282	7,580	10,960
Average Income after Taxes in Dollars	394	1,575	2,522	3,531	4,517	5,501	6,712	8,578	14,127
Consumption as % of Income after Taxes	Over 100%	Over 100%	Over 100%	Over 100%	Over 100%	96.1	93.6	88.4	77.6

Source: Calculated from Historical Statistics of the United States, Series G. 353a to G372a, "Families of two and more persons in cities of 2500 and more inhabitants," p. 26.
*Housing consists of: costs for shelter, fuel, light, refrigeration, water, household operations, furnishings and equipment. Excludes principal payments on mortgages in owned homes.

expenditures were made on these items in 1929, they accounted for only 10.3% in 1969. Also, the share of expenditures for personal business in the same period decreased from 6.5% to 5.5%, which perhaps reflects changes in the employment structure. The expenditure shares for all other groups increased. Relative increases were especially large for transportation (9.7% in 1929 versus 13.5% in 1969), due to the widespread ownership of automobiles and increase in suburban living. Expenditures for medical care rose (4.5% in 1929 versus 7.4% in 1969) because of access to better medical facilities, better information about health needs, and increased longevity. The expenditure shares for housing, household operations, personal care, and recreation increased to smaller extents. Thus during the period discussed Americans spent, in the aggregate, relatively less on basic items and more on elaborate goods and higher-quality services.

To show the relationship between consumption and personal income in the United States we present data on both, by income brackets, for the year 1960 in table 37. It is well known that a larger proportion of a low income must be spent for basic items like food and shelter. As incomes increase, more savings are made and the discretion in consumers' decisions increases. The data in table 37 cover a wide spectrum of families, ranging from the poor in the lowest income bracket, with only $1,000 annual income, to those with incomes of $10,000 and more.

The data for those with incomes over $1,000 confirm a relative decrease in food expenditures with rising incomes. (The same is true for beverages, but not for alcoholic ones.) Housing expenditures and expenditures for medical care also decrease relatively. On the other hand, when incomes rise, relatively more is spent on clothing, transportation (especially cars), recreation, and education. For those whose annual income is below $5,000, average consumption expenditures were larger than average incomes after taxes. Differences between the two had to be made up through public or private transfers, from savings, or through other means.

Gross Private Domestic Investment

Investments in capital goods are made when it is expected that it will pay to do so. Over its lifetime a capital good has a net productivity. In each time period it generates a certain revenue stream, which, when properly discounted, determines the present value of the capital good. A comparison of present value with the cost of the capital good is recommended for investment decisions. If the present value of the discounted future revenue stream exceeds the original cost, the investment is said to be worthwhile. Investment should stop if the present value is equal to cost (Keynes's marginal efficiency of capital). This is the conventional textbook criterion for investment expenditures.[6]

The making of actual investment decisions, however, is a much more complex matter. Such decisions are made under conditions of uncertainty and in many cases cannot be easily changed or reversed. What in simpler analysis is referred to as "discounting" proves in fact to be a rather intricate matter. The investor must compare expected income streams with the cost of a capital good, which is over its lifetime subject to risk. Determining expected revenue streams necessitates an estimate of the future demand for the services of the capital good. The evaluation of risk must take into consideration the possibility of physical damage to the capital good and the likelihood of premature obsolescence because of technological progress, which may permit the making of more productive and less costly capital goods.

Presumably the investor wishes to avoid risk, and one way to achieve this is to diversify his investment. He may consider several capital goods for simultaneous investment, but this confronts him with the intricate problems inherent in multiple asset choices. Additional problems arise from the liquidity effects of investments, taxation, and the expected course of future monetary policy.

Thus the investor often faces complicated asset choices, involving both subjective as well as objective factors. What may be an optimal choice for one investor may not be at all acceptable for another. The investment preferences and objectives of a small investor, for instance, may differ vastly from that of a large corporation. Heterogeneities at the micro level make it difficult to create a meaningful investment aggregate. Formally, an investment aggregate is obtained through aggregation of all investments at the micro level. Aggregation is, however, usually simple unweighed addition of investments by all micro units. The hope is, nevertheless, that the aggregate obtained proves to be stable and useful, in spite of composition problems.

For the macro-economic analysis of an economy, an aggregate investment function is needed that provides a functional relationship between aggregate private investment and the factors that are believed to determine it. Economic theory has been presented with a variety of such aggregate functions.[7] In some of these, the monetary and the real rate of interest (rate of return on capital) has been stressed, as in the Keynesian type of investment function. Other functions have focused on the accelerator relationship. Some have stressed the availability of investment funds and liquidity as an explanatory variable for investment. Though considerable theoretical and empirical work was devoted to aggregate investment functions in the United States between 1950 and 1970, much still remains to be done. The professional consensus at this time is that a satisfactory investment function does not yet exist.

The data on gross private investment in the U.S. economy provide a good picture of the structure of this large aggregate. In official statistics, gross private investment is subdivided into "fixed investment" and "changes in business inventories." Fixed investment is in turn split into "nonresidential structures," "producers' durable equipment," "nonfarm residential structures," and "farm residential structures."

Table 38 presents the structure of gross private investment for a few selected years. Gross investment consists of net investment plus replacements of worn-out buildings

TABLE 38

Gross Private Domestic Investment and Its Components,
Selected Years, 1929–70
(Dollars, Current Prices)

	1929	1940	1950	1960	1969	1970
Total Gross Private Domestic Investments of which:	16.228	13.133	54.081	74.826	139.819	135.700
(1) Nonresidential Structures	4.959	2.287	9.249	18.127	33.802 ⎫	
(2) Producers' Durable Equipment	5.601	5.262	18.654	30.283	65.510 ⎭	102.600
(3) Nonfarm Residential Structures	3.779	3.218	18.608	22.233	31.474 ⎫	
(4) Farm Residential Structures	.175	.183	.781	.614	.574 ⎭	29.700
(5) Total Fixed Investment (1)–(4)	14.514	10.950	47.292	71.257	131.360	132.300
(6) Changes in Business Inventories, Nonfarm	1.836	1.902	6.000	3.336	8.047	
(7) Changes in Business Inventories, Farm	−.122	.281	.789	.233	.412	
(8) Total Changes in Business Inventories (6) + (7)	1.714	2.183	6.789	3.569	8.459	3.500
(9) Addendum: Capital Consumption Allowance	7.868	7.503	18.342	43.408	78.858	84.300

Sources: For 1929 to 1960, *The National Income and Product Accounts of the United States, 1929–1965,* "Statistical Tables," p. 3, table 1.1. For 1969, *Survey of Current Business,* 50, no. 7 (July 1970), p. 17, table 1.1; p. 19, table 1.9. For 1970, *Statistical Abstract 1971,* p. 306, table 485; p. 309, table 492.

and equipment, that is, reinvestment. Though it would be of interest to know the actual net investment in each type of capital good, since this causes changes in the volume and composition of the capital stock, splitting gross investment into net investment and replacement for capital consumption poses considerable conceptual and methodological problems.

An existing capital stock has a quantitative as well as

qualitative dimension. It may be thought of as consisting of several layers, each embodying a certain state of technology.[8] With rapid technological progress, capital goods belonging to different layers or "vintages," may be replaced, either because they are worn out or being replaced because of premature obsolesence, by new capital goods of higher quality and greater productivity. Thus while the number of capital goods may stay the same, the productive capacity may increase. If this is the case, a good deal of all net investment actually occurs in the form of reinvestment. To what extent this will happen depends on technological advances in specific types of capital goods. Thus it is difficult to say what the actual amount of net investment is. A large part of all net investment in the United States takes the form of reinvestment. The benefits of technological progress can often be obtained only if capital goods are replaced, the earlier the better. Accelerated depreciation, giving a fiscal incentive for early replacements, may be helpful for quick "rejuvenation" of the capital stock.

It should be mentioned that public investments in the United States are not shown separately in the national income accounting statistics. Annual outlays for the construction and maintenance of roads, bridges, public buildings, etc., are contained in the item "government purchases of goods and services." The nation's annual gross domestic investment is thus larger than private gross domestic investment. To ascertain the true total of gross domestic investment, one would have to determine what share of the annual government purchases of goods and services is used for the enlargement and maintenance of the capital stock in the public domain. This should be added to private gross domestic investment.

Yet it is not only the omission of public investment that obscures the picture. Private households in the United States nowadays use many durable consumer goods that have a long economic life: houses, cars, refrigerators, washing machines, and television sets; but only houses are included in gross private domestic investment. This greatly underestimates investments in the consumer sector of the economy. The problems here stem from the well-known difficulty of determining what is production and what is consumption in an economy.

According to national income statistics, U.S. gross private domestic investment in current prices increased from a Depression low of $960 million in 1932 to $139.8 billion in 1969. But growth was not smooth. Table 34 shows how investment spending fluctuated over this period.

The bulk of all 1929–70 investment was made in fixed assets, the remainder being invested in inventories. Investments in fixed assets consist of producer durable equipment (machines, apparatuses, etc.), nonresidential structures (structures for factories, offices, etc.), and residential structures. Over the years gross investment in nonresidential structures amounted to between 55% and 70% of investment in durable equipment. A similar relationship can be found in other industrialized countries.

Investment in residential structures provides housing for the nation. In 1933, when building activity had slumped badly, its volume was a mere $563 million, a considerable decline from the $3.8 billion level in 1929. The building volume increased in subsequent years; and the 1929 level was reached again in 1941. The really great upsurge came, however, after World War II. A long-lasting building boom started to provide housing for the growing population. In 1969, residential construction reached a volume of $32 billion (table 38). With a declining farm population, only a small fraction of this investment nowadays goes into farm residential construction.

The problem of decaying inner cities and sprawling suburbs was still unsolved at the beginning of the seventies, and the demand for housing remained high. An increasing number of citizens looked for new living quarters in the suburbs. The demand for housing was often, however, a demand for low-cost housing. Yet, the private sector seems to have had difficulties in providing adequate housing at a profit for certain groups, such as the elderly and the poor. These problems also existed in other nations and have in some cases been courageously faced and tackled.[9] The United States has not yet found a satisfactory solution to low-cost housing.

Depending on the prevailing economic conditions, American inventory investments changed. They usually increased in periods of expansion and contracted in recessions. The largest annual inventory decrease, amounting to $2.48 billion, occurred in the Great Depression in 1932. The largest inventory build-up took place during the Korean War in 1951, when restocking was the desire of the day. Inventories rose in that year by $10.3 billion.

Inventories act as a useful buffer in the difficult process of synchronization between production and uses of GNP. In this function inventories can quickly reveal mistakes in business planning. Correction of such mistakes may lead to inventory adjustments which feed back on production and employment. Inventory adjustments have their own dynamics, and some economists have even talked of an inventory cycle. Inventory changes are still the most volatile component of aggregate gross investment.

Use of the Nation's Product by Government

One part of a nation's product is taken by the government to meet the demand for public goods and services that are collectively desired and must be supplied in the proper volume and composition to assure optimal economic, social, and cultural benefits. The nature of these goods and services is often such that they cannot be supplied privately, or that they can be provided privately only in an unsatisfactory manner. (This does not mean that the production of the desired items must be public. It can be private or public. A warship, for instance, can be built in a private or government shipyard).

How the resources of an economy shall be divided between private and public uses, and what kinds of public goods and services shall be produced, is in democratic societies determined through the political process.[10] Through voting and the delegation of decision-making power, people decide the use of resources in the public sector of the economy. The allocation process should be efficient and flexible because over time individual preferences and the resulting social choices with respect to the government's use of resources may change. The reasons for change can be manyfold: different needs of the economy, new social aspirations, technological developments, demographical changes, and political shifts. As a result, public expenditures—and the taxes necessary for their financing—will have to change. There is no simple rule for predicting public resource use.

The theory of public expenditure development tries to rationalize historically observed changes in the volume and structure of public resource use. Several hypotheses have been advanced, and research at the empirical level is conducted to test them.[11]

The United States national income statistics provide a record of the purchases of goods and services by the federal, state, and local governments.[12] They show a rapid growth of the volume of expenditures for goods and services during the last four decades. The structure of these changed also. All this reflects vividly the nation's fate since 1929: going through the Great Depression, fighting World War II, and coping with the aftermath of that war. It reveals the emergence of the United States as a leading economic and military power and the burdens such a role brings with it.

In 1929 the total of all government purchases of goods and services in current prices amounted to $8.5 billion. Of this, $1.3 billion was spent by the federal government and $7.2 billion by state and local governments. Purchases for national defense purposes were then low. Until 1938 they were below one billion dollars each year.[13] Thirty-two years later, in 1970, government purchases of goods and services in

TABLE 39

Government Purchases of Goods and Services
Federal, State and Local Governments, Selected Years,
1929–70
(Billion Dollars, Current Prices)

	1929	1940	1950	1960	1970
Federal Government					
Total:	1.261	6.015	18.403	53.531	99.700
of which:					
National Defense	n.a.	2.214	14.091	44.946	76.600
Other Purchases	n.a.	3.801	4.312	8.585	23.100
State and Local Governments					
Total:	7.236	7.987	19.497	46.090	120.900
Total Purchases of Federal and State and Local Government:	8.497	14.002	37.900	99.621	220.500

Sources: The National Income and Product Accounts of the United States,
1929–1965, "Statistical Tables, A Supplement to the Survey of Current Business," p. 2, table 1.1; *Statistical Abstract 1971,* p. 306, table 486.

current prices had surpassed the $220 billion mark. Of this,
nearly $100 billion was spent by the federal government,
with over $76 billion going to national defense. But because
prices rose by more than two-and-a-half times since 1929
(considering the implicit gross national product price deflator) the real increase in expenditures is less dramatic.
Indeed, absolute expenditure increases alone do not tell too
much, for they must be seen in the context of population
growth and rising incomes. Both generally lead to a demand
for larger public expenditures for civil purposes.

In addition, technological developments often require
additional public goods and services. For instance, the widespread use of the automobile in the United States in the
1920s necessitated an extensive highway construction pro-
gram. Highway expenditure was and still is a major item in
state budgets. Thus even if there had been no war and none
of the troublesome international developments after it, public expenditures still would have increased. Yet one may

TABLE 40

Government Purchases of Goods and Services
Federal, State and Local Governments, 1929–70
(Percentage Distribution)

	1929	1940	1950	1960	1970
Federal Government					
total:	14.8	43.0	48.6	53.7	45.2
of which:					
National Defense	n.a.	15.8	37.2	45.1	34.7
Other Purchases	n.a.	27.2	11.4	8.6	10.5
State and Local					
Governments total:	85.2	57.0	51.4	46.3	54.8
Total Purchases of					
Federal, State and					
Local Government:	100.0	100.0	100.0	100.0	100.0

Computed from data, table 39.

guess that the increases would have been most pronounced
at the state and local levels, which traditionally provide the
bulk of public goods for civilian use.

World War II thoroughly changed a traditional expenditure structure. In 1941 the federal government purchased
$16.9 billion in goods and services, of which $13.8 billion
were for defense. State and local governments purchased in
the same year $7.9 billion, slightly less than in the immediate
prewar years. As the nation stepped up its war effort, defense
expenditures rose dramatically. In 1944 they reached an unprecedented $87.4 billion. Concomitantly, state and local ex-
penditures had to be kept low. In 1945 they were in current
prices slightly below those in 1939; in real terms they were
much below.

The postwar question was whether there would be a
return to the old expenditure structure. The war had led to a
large federal budget and a concentration of fiscal power in
the federal government, developments which were considered not undesirable by some, but viewed with apprehension
by others. In any event, there was no return to the old expenditure pattern. Four factors seem to have worked against it.

The first was the international situation. Initial hopes

of a quick return to a peaceful postwar period vaporized after the divergences in the political aims of the great world powers became evident in the years 1946 to 1948. Later the Korean war erupted, and the nation was forced to remain in a state of military preparedness. Defense expenditures remained large, and so did the federal budgets.

Second, the upsurge of federal expenditures during the war required large federal tax revenues. To obtain these, changes in the tax structure were necessary. Many of the changes were carried over into the postwar period, and the federal revenue structure (especially the personal and corporation income taxes) continued to produce large revenues. They were so large that something like a "fiscal drag" came into existence, impeding economic growth. The federal government alone had the means to finance large projects, whereas state and local governments tried to make ends meet but frequently found themselves in financial difficulties.

Third, substantial revenues are in our times often required to achieve such technological breakthroughs as the development of atomic energy and space exploration. Since these matters are of national importance and their scale and risk will not attract private resources, the resources needed must be federally supplied.

The fourth reason for a large federal budget relates to the growth of government programs in the social field. The federal government has created additional programs in the areas of health, welfare, and education. It is to be expected that these activities will continue, notwithstanding the attempts of the Nixon administration to reverse the trend. Deeper involvement in the social problems of the nation will tend to increase the federal budget.

From World War II to 1964, federal government purchases of goods and services were above those of state and local governments, except in the year 1950. As already noted, defense expenditures bulked large in the federal budget. By 1960, $44.9 billion in goods and services were purchased for national defense. Finally, in 1965, the state and local governments caught up again, together purchasing more goods and services than the federal government. (One exception was the year 1967, which saw a sudden rise in defense expenditures because of the Vietnam war.) The ability to redirect substantial public expenditures to satisfy domestic needs depended essentially on international developments and the subsequent trend of defense expenditures. With total budgetary resources limited, international events had a considerable influence on the volume and structure of government expenditures.

The three levels of governments buy an immense variety of goods and services. Purchases range from aircraft carriers to pencils and paper clips. The national income statistics provide information on three large groups of purchases: employee compensation, purchases of structures, and purchases of other items. In 1965, for instance, 42.6% of the federal government purchases consisted of employee compensation, 5.2% purchases of structures, and 52.2% purchases of other items, which include the costly hardware modern armed forces need. In the same year, 56.7% of all state and local government purchases consisted of employee compensation, 26.4% purchases of structures, and 16.9% of purchases of other items.[14]

Thus for all levels of government combined, nearly half of all purchases consists nowadays of wages and salaries. In areas where industries have large government contracts (e.g., the aircraft industry in California) increases in government expenditures mean high incomes while decreases in expenditures bring lay-offs and unemployment. The budgets have a large effect on employment. Their aggregate as well as regional impact is of great importance and often influences spending decisions.

Foreign Transactions: Exports and Imports of Goods and Services, Transfers, and Net Foreign Investment

The United States economy is an open economy. The volume of its exports amounted to 13.9% of total world exports in

1970. In the same year its imports accounted for 12.4% of total world imports. The country was thus the largest single international trader. It was followed by West Germany (11.0% of world exports and 9.3% of world imports in 1970), the United Kingdom and Japan.[15]

The largest volume of trade occurs between developed countries. In 1970 these countries absorbed 69.1% of all U.S. exports and supplied 73.2% of all imports.[16] Among the developed countries, four have an outstanding importance for the United States' international trade: Canada, Japan, West Germany, and the United Kingdom. These countries alone bought 44% of all American exports and furnished 55.8% of all imports in 1970.

Developing countries absorbed 30% of all United States exports and supplied 26.1% of all imports in 1970. The rest of its international trade was with Communist countries and was small.[17] Thus trade with highly industrialized countries, possessing similar economic structures, is most important to the United States. They can provide the goods that are needed to complement its own production. Specialization in the production of certain types of goods and differences in taste patterns between these countries are still large enough to induce extensive trade.

The United States' volume of foreign trade, measured by exports in current prices, was about $7 billion in 1929 (table 41). During the Great Depression it dwindled to $2.4 billion (1933), and the trade volume of 1929 was not regained until the end of World War II. The 1930s had witnessed a world-wide shrinkage of trade to everyone's detriment. This trend had to be reversed, and the will to do so was there in the United States as elsewhere. Yet the situation existing in the immediate postwar years initially permitted only slow progress in the direction of trade liberalization and expansion.

The statistical time series of American exports are indicative of the growth of post-World War II trade. In 1946 exports jumped to $14.7 billion, and they grew thereafter. There were a few minor interruptions in this growth, but

TABLE 41

Foreign Transactions in the National Income and Product Accounts, Selected Years, 1929–69. (Billion Dollars, Current Prices)

	1929	1940	1950	1960	1969
Receipts from Foreigners:	7.034	5.355	13.807	27.244	55.514
(1) Exports of Goods and Services	7.034	5.355	13.807	27.244	55.514
Payments to Foreigners:	7.034	5.355	13.807	27.244	55.514
(2) Imports of Goods and Services	5.886	3.636	12.028	23.198	53.564
(3) Transfers to Foreigners					
a. Private	.343	.178	.454	.484	.784
b. Government	.034	.032	3.563	1.878	2.050
c. Total	.377	.210	4.017	2.362	2.834
(4) Net Foreign Investment	.771	1.509	−2.238	1.684	−.885
Net Exports of Goods and Services	1.148	1.719	1.779	4.046	1.950

Source: The National Income and Product Accounts of the United States, 1929–1965, "Statistical Tables," p. 74, table 4.1; Survey of Current Business 50, no. 7 (July 1970), p. 36, table 4.

these were not serious. Concomitantly there was an increase in imports, in the first years after World War II at a moderate pace, later on very much parallel to increases in exports. Until the first years of the seventies the value of exports of goods and services in peacetime always exceeded that of imports. There were surpluses on the trade account. Part of these were used by individuals and the government to make transfers to foreigners. The rest constituted net foreign investment.

Before World War II, transfers to foreigners were small. The maximum government transfer was $60 million in 1937. Personal transfers to foreigners were somewhat larger, ranging from $151 million in 1939 to $343 million in 1929. With surpluses in the trade balance and this magnitude of transfers, net foreign investment was either positive or only slightly negative. During the war the situation changed. The country needed additional resources, some of which came from abroad. Imports exceeded exports and foreign disinvestment went as high as $2.245 billion in 1943.

When the war ended in 1945, a large part of the productive facilities in other major industrial countries was destroyed, damaged, or in bad repair. Industrial and agricultural output was low. There was a threat of disease, starvation, and prolonged misery in many areas of the world. The only country that had the resources to foster rebuilding and reconstruction, and thus a return to civilized life, was the United States. The country responded to this challenge and generously gave help to other nations. The data on the country's foreign transactions between 1946 and 1951 tell the story of this massive aid.

Foreigners were eager to obtain American goods, but it was difficult for them to earn the dollars to pay for them. In many of the war-torn countries, resources were needed for reconstruction, and there were few exportables. For a new start, foreign aid from the United States was necessary. The best known among the programs implemented was the Marshall Plan. Foreign aid took several forms. A large part consisted of gifts, the rest of loans. According to national income statistics, a total of $23.2 billion was transfered to foreigners between 1946 and 1951. Of this, $19.8 billion were government transfers, the rest private ones. In the same period U.S. net foreign investment increased by $13.8 billion.

Behind all of this were large export surpluses. The international position of the U.S. economy was strong, and there was a great dollar scarcity. Some economists predicted that this scarcity would persist over a long time. Yet reconstruction abroad proceeded at a sufficiently rapid pace that exports to the United States increased and the dollar shortage disappeared earlier than expected. Indeed the international economic situation changed rapidly. Early in the sixties there were signs of a plentiful supply of dollars in countries abroad, and there was talk of a dollar glut.

From 1952 to 1969 the country's foreign transactions, as reflected in the national income statistics, showed in each year an excess of exports over imports, in some years as large as $5 billion, in others (e.g., 1953 and 1959) just a few hundred million dollars. Thus the trade balance was sound. However, the export surpluses were not large enough to permit the country to do all the other things it wished to do internationally, without running balance of payments deficits. The series of balance of payments deficits that occurred (especially in the sixties) were caused by other factors, in particular too-large government foreign grants and credits and private asset transactions for the purpose of direct foreign investment or purchases of foreign securities.

The domestic employment attributable to exports has been considerably lower in the United States than in some other countries, for example, West Germany. For the year 1966 it was estimated that a total of 65.2 million persons were privately employed in the United States. Of these, 3.1 million, or 4.7%, were employed in export industries.[18] The highest percentage of export employment existed in agriculture (11.8%) and mining (8.8%). It was followed by manufacturing (6.1%).

The composition of U.S commodity trade is a subject of special interest. It has puzzled economists and led to a reexamination of some traditional tenets of international trade theory. According to such theory, a country will export some particular types of goods and import others, a beneficial arrangement because of comparative advantages in production. Through trade, more of the domestically demanded goods can accordingly be obtained at lower cost. Comparative cost advantages in production are in turn explained by the relative abundance of particular productive factors. Abundant factors of production should, in a market economy, obtain a lower rate of return than factors that are scarcer. The hypothesis is that a country imports those goods that require for their production a large amount of the domestically scarce factor of production and little of the abundant factor. On the other hand, goods are exported that require for their production much of domestically abundant but little of the scarce factors. A country will thus augment its scarce factors of production through trade.

Traditionally, it was believed that production in the U.S. economy is, relative to many other countries, capital-intensive. The United States should therefore import labor-intensive and export capital-intensive goods. Professor Wassily Leontief tested this hypothesis with the aid of a large input-output table in 1953.[19] His conclusion was that American exports are labor-intensive and imports capital-intensive. Capital would therefore be the scarce and labor the abundant factor in the economy, a result which surprised most economists. It was labeled the "Leontief paradox." A large number of studies, theoretical as well as empirical, were subsequently made to solve the above paradox.[20]

It seems that the main reason for the paradox was the particular definition of the factors of production in Leontief's provocative study. Very few economists nowadays doubt that production in the American economy is capital intensive. Leontief's study referred to the structure of commodity trade in one particular year. Of importance also are changes over a period of time. The available data here indicate important trends. The export of food, live animals, beverages and tobacco, crude materials, and minerals and related materials showed a relative decline in the last decade. Exports of chemicals and goods falling into the general category "other manufactured goods" kept relatively constant. On the other hand, the exports of machinery and transport equipment rose dramatically. On the import side the picture is similar. Imports of food and live animals, crude materials, and mineral fuels decreased whereas imports of machinery and transportation equipment increased.[21] Thus the general trend is away from trade in crude and semifinished items. Sophisticated finished manufactured goods became more important in both exports and imports.

NOTE: A discussion of the uses of the nation's product is incomplete without an analysis of the sources and uses of gross saving. A summary of these is given in the appendix to this chapter.

Literature on Consumption Functions

Ando, A., and Modigliani, F. "The 'Life Cycle' Hypothesis of Savings: Aggregate Implications and Test." *American Economic Review* 53, no. 1 (March 1963): 55–94.

Duesenberry, J. *Income, Saving, and the Theory of Consumer Behavior.* Cambridge, Mass.: Harvard University Press, 1949.

Ferber, R. "Research on Household Behavior." In *Surveys of Economic Theory,* The American Economic Association and the Royal Economic Society, pp. 114–54. New York: St. Martin's Press, 1967.

Fisher, M. R. "Explorations in Savings Behavior." *Bulletin of the Oxford Institute of Statistics* 18, no. 3 (1956): 201–77.

Friedman, M. *A Theory of the Consumption Function.* Princeton, N.J.: National Bureau of Economic Research, Princeton University Press, 1957.

Goldsmith, R. W. *A Study of Saving in the United States.* 3 vols. Princeton, N.J.: Princeton University Press, 1955 and 1956.

Keynes, J. M. *The General Theory of Employment, Interest, and Money.* New York: Harcourt Brace, 1936.

Kuznets, S. "Proportion of Capital Formation to National Product." *American Economic Review, Papers and Proceedings* 42, no. 2(May 1952):507–26.

Leibenstein, Harvey. "Bandwagon, Snob, and Veblen Effects in the Theory of Consumer Demand." *Quarterly Journal of Economics* 64, no. 2(May 1950)183–207.

Modigliani, F., and Ando, A. "The Permanent Income and the 'Life Cycle' Hypothesis of Saving Behavior: Comparisons and Tests." In *Proceedings of Conference on Consumption and Saving,* vol. 2, edited by I. Friend and R. Jones, pp. 49–174. Philadelphia: University of Pennsylvania Press, 1960.

Smithies, A., Livingston, S. M., and Mosak, J. L. "Forecasting Postwar Demand." *Econometrica* 13, no. 1(January 1945):1–53.

Literature on Investment Functions

DeLeeuw, F. "The Demand for Capital Goods by Manufacturers: A Study of Quarterly Time Series." *Econometrica* 30, no. 3 (July 1962):407–23.

Eisner, R. "A Distributed Lag Investment Function." *Econometrica* 28, no. 1(January 1960):1–29.

Fisher, I. *The Theory Interest.* New York: Macmillan, 1930.

Fromm, G. *Tax Incentives and Capital Spending.* Washington, D.C.: The Brookings Institution, 1971.

Grunfield, Y. "The Determinants of Corporate Investment." In *The Demand for Durable Goods,* edited by A. C. Harberger, pp. 211–66. Chicago: University of Chicago Press, 1960.

Hall, R. E., and Jorgenson, D. W. "Tax Policy and Investment Behavior." *American Economic Review* 57, no. 3 (June 1967):391–414.

Hickman, B. *Investment Demand and U.S. Economic Growth.* Washington, D.C.: The Brookings Institution, 1965.

Jorgenson, D. W. "Econometric Studies of Investment Behavior." *Journal of Economic Literature* 9, no. 4(December 1971): 1111–47.

Jorgenson, D. W., and Stephenson, J. A. "Investment Behavior in U.S. Manufacturing, 1947–1960." *Econometrica* 35, no. 2 (April 1967):169–220.

Keynes, J.M. *The General Theory of Employment, Interest, and Money.* New York: Harcourt Brace, 1936.

Meyer, J. R., and Glauber, R. R. *Investment Decisions, Econometric Forecasting, and Public Policy.* Cambridge, Mass.: Harvard University Press, 1964.

Appendix to Chapter 9

The Sources and Uses of Gross Saving

The use of a nation's real product can be conveniently divided into consumption and nonconsumption, or saving. The nonconsumed part of the nation's product takes the form of different types of investment: replacement investment to offset the wear and tear of the capital stock, net investment to increase the capital stock, net foreign investment, and inventory investment. By definition, a nation's aggregate saving must be equal to aggregate investment in each time period. The national income statistics are based on this saving-investment identity.

In table 42 a summary of the sources and uses of gross saving in the U.S. economy is given for selected years. It should be observed that the data are ex-post. Without additional information, it is not possible to detect what caused the particular volumes and compositions of saving and investment. In particular, it is not known whether the actual ex-post saving and investment were close to expected saving and investment. The equality of gross saving and gross investment holds for a depressed, less-than-full-employment economy with gloomy expectations as well as for a buoyant one in which everyone is optimistic about the future. Likewise, the summary statements on the sources and uses of gross saving do not inform us as to how the gross saving was channeled into investment. In developed, industrial economies, the identity of savers and investors tends to disappear: those who make the saving decisions are generally different from those who make investment decisions. This being the case, special institutions (banks, financial intermediaries, and financial markets) are necessary to channel the saving efficiently into investment. The channeling of saving into investment is one of the functions of the financial superstructure of a market economy. In performing this function the various institutions in this structure, however, are not passive

TABLE 42

Sources and Uses of Gross Saving, Selected Years, 1929–69 (Billion Dollars, Current Prices)

	1929	1940	1950	1960	1969
1. Personal Saving	4.162	3.844	13.078	17.016	37.641
2. Noncorporate Capital Consumption Allowances	3.664	3.672	9.542	18.500	29.106
3. Total NonCorporate Gross Saving (1 + 2)	7.826	7.516	22.620	35.516	66.747
4. Undistributed Corporate Profits	2.820	3.163	16.026	13.243	23.875
5. Corporate Inventory Valuation Adjustment	.472	−.200	−4.965	.192	−5.424
6. Corporate Capital Consumption Allowances	4.204	3.831	8.800	24.908	49.752
7. Total Corporate Gross Saving	7.496	6.794	19.861	38.343	68.203
7a. Total Private Saving (3 + 7)	15.322	14.310	42.505 [a]	73.859	134.950
8. Federal Government [b] Surplus or Deficit (−)	1.175	−1.325	9.053	3.462	9.303
9. State and Local [b] Government Surplus or Deficits(−)	−.193	.638	−1.203	.220	−.649
10. Total Government [b] Surplus or Deficit(−) (8 + 9)	.982	−.687	7.850	3.682	8.654
11. Total Gross Saving	16.304	13.623	50.355	77.541	143.604
12. Gross Domestic [c] Investment	16.228	13.133	54.081	74.826	139.819
13. Net Foreign Investment	.771	1.509	−2.238	1.684	−.885
14. Gross Investment	16.999	14.642	51.843	76.510	138.934
15. Statistical Discrepancy (14 − 11)	.695	1.019	1.488	−1.031	−4.670

Sources: For 1929 to 1960, *The National Income and Product Accounts of the United States, 1929–1965,* "Statistical Tables," p. 78, table 5.1. For 1969, *Survey of Current Business* (July 1970), p. 37, table 5.1.

[a] Contains $24 million of accrued wages.
[b] Surplus and deficit in the national income and product accounts.
[c] For the components of gross domestic investment, see table 38.

agents. Their decisions on asset choices affect investment, incomes, and future savings.

The data in table 42 reveal the growth of gross saving in the U.S. economy. In current prices, gross saving increased from $16.3 billion in 1929 to $143.6 billion in 1969. Like all other national income aggregates, gross saving decreased in the Great Depression, hitting a low of $911 million in 1933. The 1929 level of gross saving was not reached again until 1940–41.

With respect to the structure of gross saving, the first distinction is between gross private saving and government saving, which are the governments' (federal, state, and local) surpluses and deficits on national income and product transactions accounts. Surpluses contribute to gross saving; deficits diminish it. In peacetime the government saving (or dissaving) is usually much smaller than gross private saving. A government surplus has a contractive effect on economic activity, whereas a deficit has an expansionary effect. The data on surpluses and deficits reflect the efforts of compensatory fiscal policy to stabilize the economy. Up to 1969, the observed range of peacetime surpluses and deficits has been from a $14.4 billion surplus (in 1947) and a $13.9 billion deficit (in 1967).

For the selected years shown in table 42, total noncorporate gross saving and total corporate gross saving were about equal in magnitude. In 1969 the former amounted to $66.7 billion, the latter to $68.2 billion.

10.
Problems and Achievements: A Summary

Like any other economy, that of the United States is, of course, not free from problems. Indeed there are plenty of them, small and great. The small problems can be expected to correct themselves and to be overcome in a normal process of adjustments. To find solutions to the great problems may require concerted actions by labor, capital, and the government. Yet all problems should be considered with perspective and understanding. It is to the credit of the country that it has paid attention to its problems and analyzed its own shortcomings. The economic education of the general public, lawmakers, and businessmen improved, as did the availability of information, during the last two decades. There is probably no other country in the world in which economic developments are so closely followed and so sharply analyzed as in the United States. Thus important economic problems are usually well known and widely discussed.

Looking back over the period 1930–70, one can discern seven great problems. The first is that of maintaining a high level of resource use and in particular a high level of employment. The second problem, closely connected with the first, is that of achieving price level stability. In the third place comes the problem of the income distribution. The fourth problem concerns the country's international economic position. The fifth problem deals with environmental effects of economic activity. The sixth problem is the maintenance of competition and consumer sovereignty. Finally, the seventh problem concerns economic decision making. Which decisions shall be private and which public ones?

These seven problems have always been present, but the emphasis given to each of them has changed. As time went on, the needs of the U.S. economy did not remain the same, nor did the actual or imagined urgency of each problem. We shall consider each of them separately.

The Problem of Full Employment

A look at the post-World War II record of the U.S. economy reveals that on the average a relatively high level of employment has been maintained. Yet this record also indicates that, with the given structure of the economy, it is difficult to decrease the unemployment rate much below 3.8% of the civilian labor force. On the other hand, appropriate fiscal and monetary policy measures seemed to be able to keep the rate below 6.2%. These figures are of no great comfort to those who give the highest priority to the attainment of full employment. Still it is gratifying to note that unemployment rates in the post-World War II period were much below those experienced in earlier times.

As much as it would be desirable for humanitarian and social reasons to decrease the rate of unemployment further, to two percent, or even one percent, it seems that this is not feasible at this time without some far-reaching institutional changes in the American economy.

The attempt to achieve a 98% or even higher level of employment by increasing aggregate demand through expansionary fiscal and monetary policy would no doubt lead to strong upward money wage and price pressures. As it is, the trade-off between increases in prices and increases in employment is such that, at high levels of employment, small increases in employment may bring with them large increases in prices. These are undesirable and derogatory to the working of the economy.

There are several types of unemployment in the U.S. economy, each having its own background and each requiring a special remedy. The first is "frictional unemployment." In an economy as complex as the American one, a certain percentage of the labor force is always reported as unemployed because of changeovers in employment. There is often a delay between leaving one employment and taking up a new one. Also, a certain time may elapse before new entrants into the labor force can find employment. Frictional unemployment is inevitable, yet it should be kept to a minimum. To this end, ready information on available employment openings and aid to persons seeking a new employment is helpful.

The second type of unemployment is of a structural nature. Unemployed persons may not be able to find work, even though there are many positions to be filled, if they are insufficiently qualified or unable to move to a place where new employment is offered. To overcome this type of unemployment is more difficult. It requires (1) an opportunity for retraining and relocation and (2) the will of the unemployed to make use of it. With rapid changes in technology, many jobs disappear each year. Indeed, in the future a person may have to retrain several times during his lifetime to stay employed. Those with few abilities and little experience will face the greatest difficulties in this process. Though programs by firms or government to facilitate retraining and readaptation to new jobs may help to overcome this problem, they are time consuming and of uncertain benefit. Helping persons to move from one location to another in order to become employed again may cut down regional structural unemployment. A good deal of the unemployment in the United States is structural.

"Cyclical unemployment" exists when the output of the economy falls below its productive capacity. Unemployment of this type was widespread during the Great Depression in the 1930s. The post-World War II recessions also brought cyclical unemployment. A deficiency in aggregate demand is the reason for this state of affairs, and stabilizing fiscal and monetary policy can help to overcome it.

From among the three types of unemployment, the structural one is the most difficult to attack. A good deal of American unemployment is of this nature. Its cure will require considerable educational efforts, and on-the-job-training programs.

The incidence of unemployment is uneven. Unemployment is higher among laborers and production workers than for professionals and white-collar workers, higher among women than men, higher among Negroes than whites, and higher among young people who first enter the labor force than those who have been working for a longer time. This incidence creates additional problems and hardships. Unemployment in the American economy has complicated structural features, and there is no simple remedy to eliminate it quickly and completely.

The Problem of Price Stability

In the history of the United States, wars have always engendered inflation. During the Civil War, World War I, and World War II price levels rose steeply, causing distortions and inequities. The Civil War and World War I were both followed by delayed, but prolonged periods of deflation that brought problems of their own.

World War II produced substantial increases in the price level. Yet, contrary to previous historical experience, there was no ensuing deflationary period. The upward movement in the price level continued, although at varying rates. Increases were large between 1945 and 1950. They remained moderate throughout the fifties and the first part of the sixties. In the latter half of the sixties the pace of inflation accelerated again. Increases in the consumer price index finally reached 5.4% in 1969 and 5.9% in 1970. This was certainly much too high a rate.

Opinions differ as to what causes inflation in the American economy. Several theories have been advanced. The first one is the traditional "demand-pull" inflation. This is sometimes characterized as "too many dollars chasing too few goods." In the period immediately following World War II and during the Korean War this type of inflation probably dominated. The problem was one of excess demand.

Another type of inflation is the "cost-push" inflation originating on the supply side. Powerful labor unions succeed in obtaining higher money wages, the costs of which are then passed on by powerful businesses in the form of higher product prices to less powerful consumers. It is argued that this process may go on even if aggregate output decreases. This would rationalize the fact that the U.S. economy has had periods of relatively high unemployment cum price level increases. According to this second theory, inflation is largely independent of the existing aggregate supply and demand situation. It has its roots ultimately in a struggle between labor and capital over income shares. This struggle takes place in a given institutional structure, and it follows its own rules. The outcome depends on a variety of factors, not the least of which is the market power of the participants involved, the strong labor unions and large corporations.

If wage demands by unions should become too large,

and if business cannot recuperate wage cost increases in markets (assuming for the moment that the monetary authorities do not increase credits to accomodate the union-business decisions on higher money wages), production may be decreased and unemployment result. If unemployment would become large enough, the increases in money wages would presumably stop.

A third factor is thus needed to permit price level increases: the monetary authorities must allow an increase in the money supply. They must, in a sense, ratify the labor-business decisions. If the monetary authorities refuse to do so, unemployment results. If they yield to political pressure and permit increases in the money supply, however, they further inflation. The issue is a difficult one. Given the objectives of a high level of employment *and* a high degree of price-level stability, the problem is that of permitting an "optimal" increase in the money supply. Achieving this is far from easy, especially if congressional policy makers should try to overcome a monetary tightness— which may be in their view unjustified—through budgetary deficits.

Traditional measures to curb inflation have not been very successful in the contemporary U.S. economy. Monetary tightness has increased unemployment, but it has not done much to decrease inflation. Thus, from time to time, the government has attempted to curb inflation through other measures. During the Kennedy and Johnson administrations, there was occasional direct interference in price-wage decisions. (The United States vs. U.S. Steel case in the Kennedy years [1962] is perhaps the best-known example.) Later on, "guidelines" for price and wage increases were issued.[1] But compliance with these was largely voluntary. The success of these guidelines in holding down inflation is uncertain. If they had any effect, it probably was not large.

The war in Vietnam, together with Lyndon Johnson's ambitious "great society" programs at home, caused substantial budgetary deficits and high rates of inflation in the second half of the 1960s. To curb these, the Nixon administration at first pursued a tight money policy in 1969-70. The effect of this was small; and in the summer of 1971 recourse was made to direct price and wage controls.

The Problem of Income Distribution

Some question whether the actual household income distribution in the contemporary United States is a socially desirable one. Those who feel that it is not argue that corrections in the existing income distribution should be implemented through public policy measures, such as changes in the progressive personal income tax (a negative income tax being one of the possibilities), income transfers, and public expenditure programs which benefit specific groups in the population.

There are two aspects to be considered in any income redistribution: the direction and extent of income changes. The direction of income redistribution should be, according to most people, from the rich to the poor, as this would reduce income inequality. Not many would take issue with this. The real problem is therefore not the direction but the extent of income redistribution. What is a "socially desirable income distribution" for guiding redistribution policies?

On this subject various strands of thinking exist. One holds that the income distribution is determined through the working of the markets in which producers and consumers try to do their best. If the markets are performing well, those who are able, enterprising, and industrious will obtain higher incomes—if not in the short-run, then in the long-run—than those who have little ability and who lack the drive to perform. Between productive efforts and rewards there exists a causal nexus that provides incentives. If there are no serious distortions in markets or outright market failures, then market solutions for income distribution can be lived with.

There are, however, certain situations in life in which a person should be entitled to public aid. Old age, sickness, accidents, the death of a husband or wife, and other calamities may seriously reduce one's ability to earn a living. There seems to be a consensus in the contemporary American society that aid should be given in such cases. The social security system, which will become more comprehensive in the future, provides incomes to many so afflicted, but other public aid may also be necessary.

Income redistribution to aid in other than hardship cases is another matter. Some argue that in the contemporary U.S. economy those whose incomes are below a certain critical level, sometimes referred to as the "poverty level," should receive income transfers. There would be a certain income level below which no one can fall. During the presidential election campaign in 1972, the Democratic candidate, Senator McGovern, talked of a guaranteed $1,000 annual income per person. This type of income redistribution would be a massive one. There are several objections to such schemes.

The first is a belief that the best way to get a person permanently out of poverty is to enable him to be productive and earn an income. Thus, income transfers as a matter of right and without any built-in incentives to become employed would not really eradicate the basic problem. Some observers even fear that such income transfers might tend to perpetuate the existing situation, making poverty a "way of life"; but this may be too pessimistic a view. Often the poor are quite willing to work, given a chance and an incentive.

The second reason for the reluctance to go into massive income distribution involves the question of who would bear the burden of the transfers. With the existing American household income distribution, the burden would fall mainly on the lower and upper middle income brackets, not on the very rich. If the large revenues necessary were to be raised through an increase in federal income taxes—in the opinion of some redistribution advocates the best revenue source for this purpose—the burden would fall heavily on taxpayers in income brackets between $8,000 and $30,000 annual gross income. Most people in these brackets feel that their federal, state, and local government taxes are quite heavy enough as it is; their resistance to tax increases planned for income redistribution purposes would be very strong.

More politically acceptable income redistribution programs seem to be those which enhance the "equal opportunity" for economic success. Programs of this type seek to improve skills and abilities of economically disadvantaged persons. Several such programs have been established in the past. How successful they will be remains to be seen.

The International Economic Situation

The political results of World War II were far reaching. The United States, Soviet Russia, and the People's Republic of China emerged as superpowers. Nations like England, France, Germany, and Japan, which had hitherto shaped the political events, became lesser powers. Ideological differences between East and West led to hostilities and a cold war. The prevailing mood in the United States after the end of hostilities in 1945, and after some further experiences in Greece, China, Berlin, and Korea, was that of resistance to the East, and the international policies of the United States became strongly influenced by the possibility of an East-West confrontation. A return to a new policy of "splendid isolation" was out of question. The country was by far the strongest in the West after the cataclysm of the war; it had become deeply involved in world affairs. Strengthening friendly countries, helping them to maintain their political independence, and aiding them with their economic problems was deemed necessary for a period of reconstruction and peaceful prosperity.

Direct economic aid in various forms was given to war-ravished countries. Efforts were made to further international economic cooperation, and a return to freer trade was favored. The United States also advocated the establishment of the European Economic Community. Once Japan and the industrialized countries in western Europe that had suffered most during World War II were back to prosperity, American attention turned towards the developing countries. Aid to these was in some years considered of great importance, and there were even plans that the richer nations should annually contribute one percent of their gross national product for this purpose.

For many years after 1945 balance of payments surpluses permitted the United States to be generous in the international economic area, without constraints on its domestic economic policy. Later U.S. international economic policy must be seen against a different background. As time went on, the situation changed. In East-West relations the cold war thawed somewhat; a concept of peaceful coexistence gradually evolved. It is true that the thaw never went far enough to permit substantial disarmaments, but the general outlook seemed friendlier. The clouds of the Cuban crisis passed, and a politically independent People's Republic of China emerged. It became clear that the Communist world, far from being a monolithic bloc, had its own grave problems. With these developments, some allies, especially France, felt that their policy objectives no longer conformed as closely as before with those of the United States. Requests by the United States that other western allies assume a larger share of the common defense burden were not received with too much enthusiasm, though cooperation continued. On the whole, the political influence of the United States in western Europe and other parts of the world became weaker.

The rebuilding and modernization of industrial capacities abroad had substantially increased productivities in the 1950s and 1960s. This, together with some notable instances of undervalued foreign currencies, under a regime of fixed exchange rates, gave foreign imports in the United States a competitive advantage. At the same time, high-cost American domestic production, together with foreign restrictions on American exports, did not permit a rapid enough rise in exports. An aggravating factor was the flow of U.S. capital abroad, the result of higher rates of interest and higher rates of return on capital abroad than at home. Yet, in spite of all of this, the country kept up substantial transfers to foreigners. The result was inevitable. Balance of payments deficits resulted, not only in one year but for several. When finally in 1971 even the trade balance turned unfavorable, it was time to take a hard look at the country's international economic situation and introduce some major adjustments. President Nixon decided to terminate the convertibility of foreign dollars claims into gold. The gold exchange standard, abandoned by other important countries long ago but kept by the United States, disappeared. Though the United States refused at first to devalue the dollar, revaluation of foreign currencies did result in a de facto devaluation. Temporary surcharges of short duration on foreign imports were introduced to help redress the balance of payments. At the same time, domestic price and wage controls were adopted to throttle domestic inflation and cut down an inflation-induced import demand.[2]

There was no denying that the country's international economic position had become weaker. Greater competitiveness of U.S. goods in foreign markets, a decrease of imports from abroad, some constraints on capital exports, and a closer scrutiny and reduction of transfers to foreigners were necessary to overcome the balance of payments problems and to end up with balance of payments surpluses. It was hoped that success along these lines would permit the dollar to fully regain its accustomed place among the hard currencies.

But how far should efforts in this direction go? The

postwar years had seen a large increase in the volume of international trade. The trade of many important countries with the United States had reached record heights. Trade had produced great benefits. It had helped to keep foreign employment, especially in countries with export-oriented economies, at a high level. Restrictive trade practices were therefore looked upon unfavorably, both at home and abroad. They would have been an abrogation of free trade principles adopted after World War II.

International trade with a minimum of restrictions presupposes, however, a coordination and harmonization of domestic economic policies. This seemed in the 1950s still a real possibility in the western world, but by the end of the 1960s there was on the whole not much progress in this area. Countries showed little enthusiasm for restrictions on their domestic economic policies if these were demanded to further international economic cooperation and coordination. There was a return to the use of policy tools which before had been considered undesirable. Floating exchange rates were approved, import surcharges were used, and in some instances there was talk of foreign exchange controls. The international economic scene seemed to have become less cooperative and harmonious.

In all of these developments, the United States has been caught between two desires. On the one hand, since prolonged deficits are intolerable, it is necessary for her to reestablish a balance of payments equilibrium. But to do this may require measures that will reduce trade and possibly hurt foreign trade partners. On the other hand, the United States has steadily advocated a movement towards freer trade, a greater international exchange of goods and services from which all can benefit. Restrictive trade practices are unpalatable. There is thus a trade-off between national and international considerations, and a choice will have to be made. What this choice will be is determined not only by the United States alone, however, but also by the attitudes of her foreign trade partners.

Environmental Effects of Economic Activity

The environmental effects of economic activities have at-
tracted much attention in the United States during the last
decade and a half. There is an increasing recognition that
modern man, given his technological capabilities, can do
great harm to the natural environment in which he lives and
on which his well-being and life ultimately depend. Air pollution in large metropolitan areas; oil spillages on the oceans,
seas and rivers; chemical and thermal pollution of large
bodies of water; dangerous radiation from nuclear devices
and experiments; and devastated tracks of land through careless strip mining exemplify the damages that can be done.
The days in which there was a comfortable reliance on the
self-regenerating powers of a benevolent nature to cure all
environmental ills have gone.

In the United States, several factors contributed to environmental problems. The growing population became a prima-
rily urban one, and clustering in urban areas occurred, bringing
with it crowding and congestion. To maintain a high standard of
living, production must be efficient, and producers are under
pressure to furnish goods and services at low cost. All too often
they are thus tempted to achieve this by shifting part of the
private cost of production onto society. For instance, instead of
installing costly cleaning devices in smokestacks to prevent air
pollution, it is less costly for the individual firm to let the smoke
escape uncleaned into the atmosphere. The environment becomes polluted, and society pays the price.

It is not only on the production side that environmental
problems arise. On the use side, contemporary American households are prodigious consumers of energy—electricity, oil,
gas, and gasoline. To furnish the vast amounts of energy
sources to meet their demands creates environmental problems; and a rising demand for them will augment the problems.
The average American consumer contributes most to pollution
when he rides in his car. Millions of gallons of gasoline and
diesel oil are burnt every day in metropolitan areas. Exhaust

fumes pollute the air, sometimes to an unbearable degree. At this time much remains to be done to overcome this problem.

Not only the petro-chemical products, gasoline and diesel oil, are a source of pollution. American industry and households nowadays use a variety of chemical products that cannot be broken up and regenerated through natural forces once they are used and discarded. Special recycling processes may be necessary to limit a lasting damage to environment from their use.

From the economic point of view, the protection of the natural environment is ultimately a cost question. There is no doubt that it is possible to effectively limit adverse environmental effects of economic activities with existing technological means. If this is done, however, the not-so-visible social cost of some present economic activities will suddenly be transformed into private cost of which everybody will be keenly aware. Production cost will increase. The consumer too may have to acquire certain types of equipment to minimize his adverse environmental impact. Ultimately there are two problems: Who will carry the burden of all these measures? Who will benefit from them? And *how* clean an environment does society wish to have, given the inevitable cost (and probably steeply rising cost if the environmental aspirations become more ambitious) required to provide it? Should concern over environmental effects be permitted to interfere with other policy objectives? For instance, should we forego some economic growth to save the environment? There are evidently trade-offs and choices that will have to be made.

Competition and Consumer Sovereignty

If a market economy is to perform properly it should be competitive and consumers should be free and sovereign in their choices. Yet the question of how competitive the U.S. economy is and to what degree consumer sovereignty exists, is a moot one. The situation is the same as in other contemporary market economies: the market form of pure or perfect competition is rare, and the consumer's tastes and choices are often formed in response to external factors over which he has little or no influence.

In the terminology of micro-economics, most markets in the U.S. economy are imperfect competition markets. They are monopolistic or oligopolistic. On the supply and demand side, important economic units (corporations, labor unions, etc.) are often of a large size and possess much more market power than they should have under pure (or perfect) competition. It is true that these large units do "compete" with each other, but the nature of this "competition" is different from that in perfectly competitive markets; it has never been fully explained nor understood. There is, for instance, no consensus on precisely what large firms are maximizing, how they form expectations, and what strategies they use to achieve their objectives. Many students doubt that short-run profit maximization is the target. Long-run profit maximization may be the ultimate aim, but what are the preconditions for this? Will a firm put its main efforts in maintaining a given market share, or will it go for sales maximization to assure long-run profit maximization? Will the attitude of management be "satisficing" rather than "maximizing"? On the other side, what are the aims and objectives of large labor unions? What determines their strategies and actions? Much is still to be learned about all of this.

The power of the U.S. economy resides in its industry, and in industry the core is made of the large corporations and labor unions. What is decided by these large entities profoundly affects the economic fate of the nation. Since developments in this core have wide repercussions and are therefore of public interest, the federal government takes a keen interest in wage negotiations between corporations and unions, and it closely follows corporate price decisions. Big business, big labor unions, and big government nowadays determine what is going to happen to wages and prices and, one step further removed, to employment and price level changes.

In important sectors of the economy "perfect competition" in the neoclassical sense does not exist. One tries to find solutions to economic problems through a kind of "concerted action of the social partners, business and labor," with government watching that the general public is not short-changed. The decision-making process in the very core of the economy has evolved in this direction, and it is difficult to see how it could be reversed. A return to something like "perfect competition" through a breaking up of large corporations and labor unions, as is occasionally suggested by some economists, is a pious wish and ignores the realities of American economic life. Large corporations and large unions evolved historically, they are part of the economy, and—barring far-reaching, fundamental, institutional changes—they are going to stay.

Connected with economic decision making is the concept of consumer sovereignty, one of the most cherished ideas of neoclassical economic theory. It stipulates that the consumer must be free to choose, subject to a given budget constraint, that bundle of goods and services from which he will derive the greatest satisfaction. He is supposed to make his choices intelligently and rationally, being able to do so because he has all the necessary information. According to theory, his preferences and tastes are "givens" and are not responsive to outside efforts to change them in this or that direction.[3]

Such assumptions are tenuous. They are certainly unrealistic for consumers in the contemporary U.S. economy. Many of the commodities the modern consumer needs are sophisticated and elaborate. Often he does not possess the ability to determine precisely what product is best for his needs. He must rely on such information as he can obtain through advertisements, salesmen, or consumer experts. Once he has this information he may then opt to choose from among a sometimes rather limited number of standardized products.

To overcome this consumer handicap, efforts to increase relevant consumer information are necessary. In case of deficiencies and failures in products he has bought, the consumer should of course be adequately protected. As it is now he is often in a weak position and on the defensive.

Another intricate problem is the manipulation of preferences and tastes of consumers in the U.S. economy. Conventional economic theory holds that if a producer develops a product, he will take into account the variety of tastes and preferences of consumers to assure sales. Existing products usually already cater to these given tastes and preferences, however. Thus the producer may decide to produce something that is actually or supposedly "new." He will indicate that his is an "avant garde" product. The risk, however, is that the product may not appeal if it is simply put onto the market without having had special attention drawn to it. The novel product could become a failure. To avoid this, massive advertisement may be launched, stating the new product's actual or supposed advantages and its superiority over existing ones. A product image may thus be created, and consumer preferences and tastes may be changed. Thus the production process begins to shape the demand, which is a serious matter, certainly one alien to neoclassical economic theory.

Through newspapers, magazines, radio, roadside advertisements, and especially television, the average American consumer is exposed to advertising, some useful and informative, but much of it simply irrelevant, high-pressure salesmanship by which tastes and preferences are influenced and shaped, for good or bad. It is very difficult to say how sovereign the consumer in the contemporary U.S. economy actually is.

Private Preferences and Public Choices

In a democracy, private preferences ultimately determine under what type of government the people wish to live and how this government shall work. Individual preferences underlie public choices by the government. There is no "Staat an sich," a government which has the power to make choices independently of the will and wishes of the people. An "organische Staatstheorie" (a theory that government is some organic or unitary being acting independently of its citizens) has little appeal to free people in a democracy. The idea that individual preferences ultimately determine public choices is a cherished one in the United States, with deep roots in the country's history.

The American citizen expresses his economic preferences in two ways, in the market place through his dollar vote and through his ballot in public elections. With the former vote he influences markets directly, with his latter vote he exerts an influence through the political process. Both votes should be compatible for the rational individual. If he thinks that the private economy can handle an economic problem better than the public economy, he will favor private activities in his market vote and be against public activities in the same area in his political vote, and vice versa. Thus decisions on what type of economic activities shall be performed in the private sector and what types in the public sector will be made. Depending on individual economic and social positions, opinions on this will vary. Some may prefer to see the government assume a greater role in the nation's economic life, while others may feel that its role is already too large. What, then, is the proper role of government in the American economy?

Ideas about this role have changed greatly since the turn of the century. Originally the government had in normal times scarcely any greater responsibility than to see to it that the framework of market economy was safeguarded. National defense, maintenance of law and order, control of monopolies and trusts, and avoidance of inflation and deflation were the main tasks. The rest could be entrusted to the working of the market. Today many changes have occurred. The government is deeply involved in a variety of areas affecting the economic welfare of the nation. The public expects that the government will try to move the economy as near as possible to full employment, that it will maintain price level stability, and that it will see to it that a socially acceptable income distribution emerges. In addition there are many other problems, nationwide or local, in which the government is supposed to help. During the last two decades Americans began increasingly to look towards the federal government for the solution of economic and social problems—although the wisdom of this has now been questioned.

There may be a "law of increasing economic activity of the state." Perhaps, perhaps not. Yet government in a market economy cannot become involved in an ever-increasing number of economic problems. There are limits to what it can do and what it should do in the economic field. More and larger government programs will lead to larger budgets—which are already increasing each year with existing programs—and these will require even larger tax revenues. As government programs increase, private decision-making must decline.

Those who reason in terms of social cost and benefits of new government programs usually abstract from the cost of the shrinkage of the domain of private decision making. True enough, in some cases this may be small, yet the cost is there. For many Americans, it is a permanent erosion of fundamental principles and values. Others seem to consider it as a healthy process towards a better society.

The problem of private preferences and social choices in the contemporary American economy runs deep. With the ever-increasing complexity and scope of economic problems it will remain an area in which many soul-searching questions must be asked.

A Last Word: The Achievements

In spite of its problems, the U.S. economy is a large and powerful one. It is a dynamic economy in which change, adjustment, and adaptation to new conditions and technological advances are permanent features. It relies basically on incentives and initiatives to galvanize productive efforts and generate economic growth. At the same time it is an economy in which attention is given to equity problems. Market forces are tempered and restrained when the welfare of the population requires it. In its nature the American economy is not a pure market economy. It certainly is not a "laissez faire" market economy. On the other hand, it has nothing in common with the "planned economies" as they exist in other parts of the world.

A large private sector, in which the bulk of all economic activities occurs, is complemented by a smaller public sector. What is done in the economy is determined by private and public preferences, through market decisions and political decisions.

The production of the U.S. economy is the largest in the world. The country has the highest per capita income. Never before in history have so many of a nation's people enjoyed such a high standard of living as in the contemporary United States.

Everything considered, the economy performed well after World War II. It solved the basic input-output distribution problem, faced by all economies, reasonably well, with minimum interferences in the choices of individuals. Everyone was free to decide in what ways to earn his income and how to use it. In a time when freedom of economic choice has become severely restricted or even abolished in some other powerful contemporary countries, it is well to remember this.

Some critics proclaim that the solutions the economy provided were not really satisfactory. More was expected. In some instances these claims were justifiable; in many others they were not. Expectations were often too high. It was frequently forgotten, especially in the second part of the 1960s, that no economy can do all things at once, given the constraints under which it has to operate.

In the first two years of the 1970s the outlook for the U.S. economy was a reasonably good one. It had once more proved itself as rugged and resilient. By the end of 1972 it was about to shrug off the difficulties that had beset it in the second half of the sixties and was ready for another period of vigorous expansion, though some clouds were on the horizon. America relied on its powerful economy for a continued prosperity, which promised to be a prosperity with peace abroad and at home.

Notes

Chapter 1

1. U.S. Bureau of Census, *Statistical Abstract of the United States: 1971* (Washington, D.C., 1971), p. 11, table 9. Increases as percentage of 1960 population.

2. The "center of population" is defined as that point upon which the United States would balance, if it were a rigid plane without weight and if each individual in the population distributed thereon is assumed to have equal weight and to exert an influence on a central point proportional to his distance from that point.

3. *Statistical Abstract 1971*, p. 11, table 10.

4. *Statistical Abstract 1971*, p. 8.

5. *Statistical Abstract 1971*, pp. 30, 31.

6. Calculated from *Statistical Abstract 1971*, p. 27, table 27.

7. *Statistical Abstract 1971*, p. 24.

8. *Statistical Abstract 1971*, p. 26, table 26.

9. *Statistical Abstract 1971*, p. 36, table 44.

10. *Statistical Abstract 1971*, p. 37, table 45.

11. *Statistical Abstract 1971*, p. 37, table 46.

12. *Statistical Abstract 1971*, p. 37, table 46.

13. The so-called Eastern population corridor between Boston and Washington and the region between Akron and Cleveland, Ohio and Flint, Michigan could become such super urban agglomerations.

14. All figures are from *Statistical Abstract 1971*, p. 16, table 14.

15. All figures are from *Statistical Abstract 1971*, p. 100, table 147.

16. *Statistical Abstract 1971*, p. 104, table 153.

17. All percentages were computed from *Statistical Abstract 1971*, p. 103, table 151.

18. *Statistical Abstract 1971*, p. 111, table 167.

Chapter 2

1. Land can be either treated as a given, nonreproducible asset without net productivity or as a very long-lived capital good. In the latter case it could be included in capital.

2. An example of such a production function is the constant elasticity of substitution (CES) production function, with its special cases.

3. All figures are from *Statistical Abstract 1971*, p. 210, table 327. Population figures refer to total noninstitutional population.

4. *Statistical Abstract 1967*, p. 218, table 307.

5. *Statistical Abstract 1971*, p. 210, table 327; p. 211, table 328.

6. The participation rate is defined as the number of people of an age bracket in the labor force divided by the total number of people in that bracket.

7. *Statistical Abstract 1971*, p. 210, table 327.

8. *Statistical Abstract 1967*, p. 218, table 307.

9. For a definition of SMSA see *Statistical Abstract 1971*, p. 2.

10. *Statistical Abstract 1971*, p. 211, table 329.

11. For a short survey of the growth of American unionism, see: Lloyd G. Reynolds, *Labor Economics and Labor Relations*, 4th ed. (Englewood Cliffs, N.J.: Prentice Hall, 1965), pp. 25–51.

12. *Statistical Abstract 1971*, p. 233, table 368. The number is based on dues-paying members. Not included are members in single-firm and local unaffiliated unions.

13. *Statistical Abstract 1971*, p. 233, table 369.

Chapter 3

1. All figures are from U.S. Department of Commerce, Bureau of Census, *Pocket Data Book, U.S.A.* (Washington, D.C., 1971), p. 78, table 60; p. 79, table 62.

2. *Statistical Abstract 1971*, p. 328, table 524.

3. *Pocket Data Book, U.S.A.*, 1971, p. 79, table 62; p. 234, table 337.

4. *Statistisches Jahrbuch 1971*, p. 54.

5. *Pocket Data Book, U.S.A.*, 1971, p. 213.

6. *Statistical Abstract 1971*, p. 626, table 1027.

7. *Statistical Abstract 1971*, p. 168, table 271.

8. For a discussion of the problems involved, see: U.S., Congress, Senate, Committee on National Water Resources, *Water Resources Activities in the United States*, 1960.

9. *Statistical Abstract 1971*, p. 497, table 784 and p. 503, table 796.

10. The interested reader can find ample information on this subject in: U.S. Department of Interior, Bureau of Mines, *Minerals Yearbook*, annual, issued in 3 vols.

11. *Enclyclopedia Britannica,* 1970, s.v. "Coal and Coal Mining."

12. All figures are from *Statistical Abstract 1971,* p. 642, table 1049. Recalculated into metric tons.

13. *Statistical Abstract 1971,* p. 643, table 1052. Proved reserves are those which are known to exist and can be economically recovered at current prices and by current methods. The actual reserves are probably much larger.

14. *Statistical Abstract 1971,* p. 644, table 1053.

15. *Statistical Abstract 1971,* p. 647, table 1056.

16. *Statistical Abstract 1971,* p. 650, table 1069.

17. *Statistical Abstract 1971,* p. 649, table 1068.

18. *Statistical Abstract 1971,* p. 648, tables 1064–67.

Chapter 4

1. Simon Kuznets, *Capital in the American Economy: Its Formation and Financing,* A study by the National Bureau of Economic Research (Princeton, N.J.: Princeton University Press, 1961), p. 15.

2. The great economist Joseph A. Schumpeter once suggested that it might be useful to think of the total of all capital goods in their particular structure as a matrix. This would have to be a dynamic matrix however. As time passes some of its elements vanish. Also the size of the matrix might have to change. See J. A. Schumpeter, *History of Economic Analysis,* (New York: Oxford University Press, 1963), p. 900.

3. See, for instance, Robert M. Solow, *Capital Theory and the Rate of Return,* Professor Dr. F. De Vries Lectures (Amsterdam: North-Holland Publishing Co., 1963); Joan Robinson, *The Accumulation of Capital,* (Homewood, Ill: 1956), Richard D. Irwin, pp. 103–5 and 117–23.

4. It is evidently out of the question to use the monetary rate of interest for capitalization purposes. Each change of interest by the monetary authorities would change the value of the country's capital stock.

5. *Pocket Data Book, U.S.A.* (1971), p. 205, table 284. The growth is found with the compound interest formula.

6. *Ibid.*

Chapter 5

1. Joseph A. Schumpeter's theory of innovating entrepreneurs is the best example. For another, more recent, effort to assign to technological progress the prime role in the growth process of a capitalistic economy, see Nicholas Kaldor and James A. Mirrless, "A New Model of Economic Growth," *Review of Economic Studies* 29 (June, 1962): 174–92.

2. See, for instance, Edward F. Denison, *The Sources of Economic Growth in the United States and the Alternative Uses Before Us,* Supplementary Paper no. 13 (New York: Committee for Economic Development, 1962), p. 230.

3. All figures are from *Statistical Abstract 1971,* p. 517, table 821.

4. A scientist was defined as a person who is engaged in scientific and engineering work at a level requiring a knowledge of science equivalent at least to that acquired through completion of a four-year college course. *Statistical Abstract 1971,* p. 508.

5. This figure refers to full-time and part-time personnel but excludes graduate students doing part-time service. All figures are from *Statistical Abstract 1971,* pp. 508–17, various tables.

6. *Statistical Abstract 1971,* p. 508, table 800; p. 509, table 801.

7. *Statistical Abstract 1971,* p. 510, table 804.

Chapter 6

1. For a discussion of the conceptual problems connected with national income accounting, see Richard and Nancy D. Ruggles, *National Income Accounts and Income Analysis* (New York: McGraw-Hill, 1956);. U.S. Department of Commerce, Office of Business Economics, *National Income* (1954 ed.); and *U.S. Income and Output* (1958). These are supplements to the *Survey of Current Business,* published by the U.S. Department of Commerce. A further source is the U.S. Department of Commerce, Office of Business Economics, *The National Income and Product Accounts of the United States, 1929–1965.* For national income data for the years 1966–69, see U.S. Department of Commerce, *Survey of Current Business* (July 1970 issue).

2. John Maynard Keynes, *The General Theory of Employment Interest and Money* (New York: Harcourt, Brace and Co., n.d.)

3. More recent data show a decline from $725.6 billion in 1969 to $722.1 billion 1970.

4. The average annual compounded rates of change in GNP were as follows: 1940–46, 5.5%; 1945–51, 1.3%; 1950–61, 3.1%; 1960–66, 5.1%; and 1965–69, 4.2%. *Statistical Abstract 1971,* p. 307, table 487.

5. Adolph Wagner, "Three Extracts on Public Finance," translated from the German in *Classics in the Theory of Public Finance,* edited by R.A. Musgrave and A.T. Peacock (New York: Macmillan, 1958), pp. 1–15.

6. *Statistical Abstract 1971,* p. 459, table 710.

7. Gross receipts are defined as receipts from sales and services less allowances, rebates and returns, excluding capital gains or losses and investment income not associated with the taxpayer's business. *Statistical Abstract 1971,* p. 461, table 715, n. 2.

8. Computed from *Statistical Abstract 1971*, p. 459, table 711, and p. 460, table 713.

9. Source: *Statistical Abstract 1971*, p. 459, table 711.

10. *Statistical Abstract 1971*, p. 459, table 710.

11. *Statistical Abstract 1971*, p. 459, table 711.

12. *Statistical Abstract 1971*, p. 460, table 713.

13. See, for instance "The 500 Largest U.S. Industrial Corporations," *Fortune Directory* (15 June 1968).

14. *Statistical Abstract 1971*, p. 467, table 729.

15. For a discussion of the role of corporations in modern society, see Edward S. Mason, *The Corporation in Modern Society* (Cambridge: Harvard University Press, 1959). More recently the problem has been discussed by John Kenneth Galbraith in his controversial book *The New Industrial State*, paperback ed. (New York: The New American Library, 1968).

Chapter 7

1. For a method to split labor income into "simple wages" and a "return to human capital," see Karl W. Roskamp and Gordon C. McMeekin, "Factor Proportions, Human Capital and Foreign Trade: The Case of West Germany Reconsidered," *The Quarterly Journal of Economics* 82 (February 1968):152–60.

2. Some personal income distributions use "spending units" or "adult units," specially defined micro units that may be even more useful.

3. For the derivation of alternative incomes for the U.S. economy in this context, see R. A. Musgrave, "The Incidence of the Tax Structure and its Effects on Consumption," in *Federal Tax Policy for Economic Growth and Stability*, Joint Committee Print, 84th Congress, (Washington, D.C., November 9, 1955).

4. The U.S. statistics on personal income distribution distinguish "households," "families," and "unrelated individuals." These units are defined as follows: A "household" consists of all persons who occupy a housing unit. It includes the related family members and all unrelated persons, if any. A person living alone in a housing unit, or a group of unrelated persons sharing a housing unit as partners, is also counted as a household. The term "family" refers to a group or two or more persons related by blood, marriage, or adoption and residing together; all such persons are considered as members of the same family. The term "unrelated individuals" refers to persons fourteen years old and over (other than inmates of institutions) who are not living with any relatives. An unrelated individual may constitute a one-person household by himself, or he may be part of a household including one or more families or unrelated individuals, or he may reside in group quarters such as a rooming house. For further details, see U.S. Department of Commerce, *Cur-*

rent Population Reports, Consumer Income Series, p. 60, no. 80
(October 4, 1971), p. 5–6.

5. For a quantitative measure of income inequality, the Gini
coefficient is often used. We shall call it G and refer for its explanation to figure 7. G is found by dividing the area between the diagonal
and the observed curve AB by the area of the triangle ABC. The
range of values for G is given by $0 \leq G \leq 1$. $G = 0$ implies perfect
income equality. $G = 1$ signifies complete inequality. For the
United States personal income distribution G was smaller in 1962
than in 1929.

Chapter 8

1. Savings can of course also be used for human capital formation. In this context, however, we are concerned only with
nonhuman capital formation and wealth.

2. "Survey of Financial Characteristics of Consumers," *Federal Reserve Bulletin* (March 1964), p. 285.

3. U.S. Treasury Department, Internal Revenue Service,
Statistics of Income, 1962 Supplemental Report, Personal Wealth.

4. Robert J. Lampman, *The Share of Top Wealth-Holders in
National Wealth 1922–56.* A study by the National Bureau of Economic Research (Princeton, N.J.: Princeton University Press, 1962).

5. Table 33 shows relatively high stock holdings by the lowest income bracket. This can be explained by the presence of old or
retired people in this bracket who own stock and receive dividend
income. More stocks are owned by this income bracket than would
be expected.

6. See, for instance, Milton Friedman and Leonard J. Sav-
age, "Utility Analysis of Choices involving Risk," *The Journal of
Political Economy,* 56 (August 1948):279–304.

7. Spending units are roughly equivalent to households.
These and the following figures are estimated from Lampman, p.
232 (chart 37) and p. 228, table 107.

8. Lampman, p. 212, chart 34.

9. *Statistical Abstract of the United States 1971,* p. 327,
tables 522 and 523. Further source: U.S., Treasury Department, Internal Revenue Service, *Statistics of Income, 1962,* Supplemental
Report, Personal Wealth.

Chapter 9

1. "Production" in this case comprises domestic production
and "production" through trade. The country can enjoy a larger
national product with trade than without trade; thus the latter is
productive.

2. For two large, sophisticated models see J. S. Duesenberry, G. Fromm, L. R. Klein, and E. Kuh, eds., *The Brookings*

Quarterly Econometric Model of the United States Economy (Chicago: Rand-McNally, 1965) and Michael K. Evans and Lawrence R. Klein, *The Wharton Econometric Forecasting Model,* 2d enlarged ed. (Philadelphia: Economics Research Unit, Wharton School of Finance and Commerce, University of Pennsylvania, 1968).

3. Simon Kuznets, *National Product since 1869* (1946), pp. 35, 36, 41, 46, 52. Data is given in R. A. Gordon, *Business Fluctuations* (New York: Harper and Bros., 1952), p. 368, table 20.

4. See George Katona, *The Powerful Consumer* (New York: McGraw-Hill, 1960) and the sources listed, pp. 265–71. Important research on consumer behavior was conducted at the Survey Research Center of the University of Michigan by George Katona, J. B. Lansing, J. N. Morgan, and their collaborators.

5. John Maynard Keynes, *The General Theory of Employment Interest and Money,* American ed. (New York: Harcourt, Brace and Co., n.d.) p. 96.

6. See, for instance, Erich Schneider, *Wirtschaftlichkeitsrechnung* (Tübingen: J.C.B. Mohr[Paul Siebeck], 1951), pp. 1–32.

7. See "Literature on Investment Functions" at end of Chapter 9.

8. On this problem see Robert M. Solow, *Capital Theory and the Rate of Return* (Amsterdam: North Holland Publishing Co., 1963).

9. For instance, the large West German "Sozialer Wohnungsbau" after 1949. See Karl W. Roskamp, *Capital Formation in West Germany* (Detroit: Wayne State University Press, 1965), pp. 176–82.

10. See Alan T. Peacock, "Fiscal Means and Political Ends," in *Essays in Honor of Lionel Robbins,* edited by Maurice Peston and Bernhard Corry (London, 1972) and Karl W. Roskamp, "Multiple Fiscal Policy Objectives and Optimal Budget: A Programming Approach," *Public Finance* 26, no. 2 (1971): 361–74. For a comparison of the resource allocation problems in capitalist and socialist economies, see R. A. Musgrave, "Tax Policy under Decentralized Socialism, A Summary," *Public Finance* 23, nos. 1,2 (1968): 203–11. For a discussion of problems encountered in underdeveloped countries, see Wolfgang F. Stolper, "Planung Preise und Löhne," in *Verstehen und Gestalten der Wirtschaft, Festgabe für Friedrich A. Lutz* (Tübingen: J. C. B. Mohr [Paul Siebeck], 1971), pp. 337–56.

For a discussion of the problem of the relationship between individual and social preferences, see Karl W. Roskamp and Gordon C. McMeekin, "The Symmetry Approach to Committee Decisions: An Empirical Study of a Local Government Budget Committee," *Zeitschrift für die Gesamte Staatswissenschaft* 126(January 1970):75–96, and the literature cited therein.

11. See R. A. Musgrave, *Fiscal Systems,* (New Haven, Conn.: Yale University Press, 1969), pp. 69–124; Adolph Wagner, "Staat in nationalökonomischer Hinsicht," in *Handwörterbuch der Staats-*

wissenschaften, vol. 7 (Jena: Gustav Fischer Verlag, 1911), 727–39, reprinted in H.C. Recktenwald, ed., *Finanztheorie* (Köln, Berlin, 1969); Alan T. Peacock and Jack Wiseman, *The Growth of Public Expenditure in the United Kingdom* (Princeton, N.J.: National Bureau of Economic Research, Princeton University Press, 1961); M. Copeland, *Trends in Government Financing* (Princeton, N.J.: National Bureau of Economic Research, Princeton University Press, 1961); R. A. Musgrave and J. M. Culbertson, "The Growth of Public Expenditures in the United States 1890–1948," *National Tax Journal* (June 1953); and H. T. Oshima, "Share of Government in Gross National Product for Various Countries," *American Economic Review* (June 1957).

    12. The statistics record "income and product transactions" of the governments. These are smaller than budget totals, which include, besides "income and product transactions," other, nonincome generating items, e.g. transfer payments, grants-in-aid, and proceeds from the sale of assets.

    13. Direct expenditures for military services were $702 million in 1932, $541 million in 1934, and $916 million in 1936. *Historical Statistics of the United States, Colonial Times to 1957,* Series Y, 484–516, p. 725.

    14. U.S. Department of Commerce, *The National Income and Product Accounts of the United States, 1929–65,* pp. 53 and 55, tables 3.1 and 3.3.

    15. *Statistisches Jahrbuch für die Bundesrepublik Deutschland 1971,* p. 71.

    16. These and the following figures are computed from *Statistical Abstract 1971,* p. 768, table 1241.

    17. Less than one percent of all exports and imports in 1970.

    18. *Statistical Abstract 1971,* p. 775, table 1245.

    19. Wassily Leontief, "Domestic Production and Foreign Trade: The American Capital Position Re-examined," in *Proceedings of the American Philosophic Society* (Autumn 1953), p. 343.

    20. For discussions of the Leontief paradox, see Gottfried Haberler, "A Survey of International Trade Theory," translated from the German and reprinted in *Special Papers in International Economics,* no. 1 September 1955 (Princeton, N.J.: International Finance Section, Department of Economics and Sociology, Princeton University Press, 1955), pp. 22–25, and Jagdish Bhagwati, "The Pure Theory of International Trade," *The Economic Journal* (March 1964), pp. 21–25, and sources given in this article on pp. 78–80. For a study of West German factor proportions and foreign trade, see Karl W. Roskamp, "Factor Proportions and Foreign Trade: The Case of West Germany," *Weltwirtschaftliches Archiv,* no. 2 (1963), pp. 319–26, and Karl W. Roskamp and Gordon C. McMeekin, "Factor Proportions, Human Capital and Foreign Trade: The Case of West Germany Reconsidered," *The Quarterly Journal of Economics* (February 1968), pp. 152–60.

21. *Statistical Abstract 1971*, pp. 772 and 777, tables 1242 and 1247.

Chapter 10

1. For problems connected with such guidelines see George P. Schulz and Robert Z. Aliber, eds., *Guidelines* (Chicago: The University of Chicago Press, 1966). Includes contributions by Gardner Ackley, Robert M. Solow, Milton Friedman, John T. Dunlop, Harry G. Johnson, and others.

2. This was not the end of adjustment measures; by 1973 the dollar had been devalued twice.

3. Neoclassical economic theory does not have much to say about the formation of tastes. This shortcoming was severely criticized by Kenneth E. Boulding in "Economics as a Moral Science," (AEA presidential address 1968), *The American Economic Review* (March 1969), especially pp. 1 and 2.

Bibliography

Selected Official Publications*

Board of Governors of the Federal Reserve System. *Federal Reserve Bulletin*. Washington, D.C.: Division of Administrative Services. Published monthly.
———. *Flow of Funds Accounts, 1945–1968*. Washington, D.C., March 1970.
———. *Historical Chart Book*. Issued annually in September.
Cabinet Task Force on Oil Import Control. *The Oil Import Question: A Report of the Relationship of Oil Imports to the National Security*. Washington, D.C., 1970.
Commission on Foreign Economic Policy. *Staff Papers*. Washington, D.C.: U.S. Government Printing Office, February 1954. 531 p.
Economic Report of the President, together with *The Annual Report* of the Council of Economic Advisers. Published annually.
National Commission on Urban Problems. *Building the American City*. Report of the National Commission on Urban Problems to the Congress and the President of the United States. House Document no. 91-34. Washington, D.C., 1968.
U.S. Congress, Joint Committee on the Economic Report. *Monetary Policy and the Management of the Public Debt, Their Role in Achieving Price Stability and High-Level Employment* (Patman Report). 82d Cong., 2d sess., no. 123, pt. 1. Washington, D.C., 1952.
———. *Federal Tax Policy for Economic Growth and Stability*. 84th Cong., 1st sess., 9 November 1955. 929 p.
U.S. Congress, Joint Economic Committee. *Staff Report on Employment, Growth, and Price Levels*. 86th Cong., 1st sess., 24 December 1959. Washington, D.C., 1960.
———. *State of the Economy and Policies for Full Employment*. 87th Cong., 2d sess., August 1962.
U.S. Department of Commerce, Bureau of Census. *Census of Manufactures*. Published quarterly.

———. *Historical Statistics of the United States, Colonial Times to 1957: A Supplement to the Statistical Abstract of the United States.* Washington, D.C., 1960.

———. *Historical Statistics of the United States: Continuation to 1962 and revisions.* Washington, D.C., 1965.

———. *Statistical Abstract of the United States.* Published annually.

U.S. Department of Commerce, Office of Business Economics. *Survey of Current Business.* Published monthly.

———. *The National Income and Product Accounts of the United States, 1929–1965, Statistical Tables: A Supplement to the Survey of Current Business.* Washington, D.C., 1966.

U.S. Department of Health, Education, and Welfare. *Vital Statistics of the United States.* Published annually.

U.S. Department of Labor, Bureau of Labor Statistics. *Employment and Earnings and Monthly Report of the Labor Force.* Published monthly.

———.*Monthly Labor Review.* Provides consumer price index, city average indexes, and the wholesale price index.

U.S. Department of the Treasury, Internal Revenue Service. *Corporation Income Tax Returns.* Published annually.

———. *Personal Wealth Estimated from Estate Tax Returns.* Washington, D.C., 1962. 103 p.

———. "Individual Income Tax Returns." *Statistics of Income.* Published annually with historical summary in each issue.

*These documents available from Superintendent of Documents, U.S. Government Printing Office, Washington, D.C.

Other Books

Abramovitz, Moses. "Economics of Growth." In *A Survey of Contemporary Economics,* edited by Bernhard F. Haley, vol. 2, pp. 132–78, and the sources cited there. Homewood, Ill.: Richard D. Irwin, Inc., 1952.

Adams, Walter, ed. *The Brain Drain.* New York: Macmillan Co., 1968.

Bowen, William G., Harbison, Frederick H., Lester, Richard A., and Somers, Herman M., eds. *The American System of Social Insurance: Its Philosophy, Impact, and Future Development.* New York: McGraw-Hill, 1968.

Brown, William Adams. *The United States and the Restoration of World Trade.* Washington, D.C.: Brookings Institution, 1950.

Brown, William Adams, and Opie, Redvers. *American Foreign Assistance.* Washington, D.C.: Brookings Institution, 1953.

Carter, Anne P. *Structural Change in the American Economy.* Harvard Studies in Technology and Society. Cambridge, Mass.: Harvard University Press, 1970.

Caves, Richard. *American Industry: Structure, Conduct, Perfor-mance.* Englewood Cliffs, N.J.: Prentice Hall, 1964.

Chamberlain, Neil W. *The Labor Sector: An Introduction to Labor in the American Economy,* New York: McGraw-Hill, 1965.

The Commission on Money and Credit. *Inflation, Growth and Em-ployment* and *Stabilization Policies.* 2 vol. of 18 dealing with U.S. financial institutions and monetary and fiscal policy. En-glewood Cliffs, N.J.: Prentice-Hall, 1963.

Davis, Lance E., and North, Douglass C. *Institutional Change and American Economic Growth.* New York: Cambridge Univer-sity Press, 1971.

Denison, Edward F. *The Sources of Economic Growth in the United States and the Alternatives before Us.* Supplemen-tary Paper no. 13. New York: Committee for Economic De-velopment, 1962.

Dernburg, Thomas F., and McDougall, Ducan. *Macroeconomics.* 4th ed. New York: McGraw-Hill, 1972.

Dewhurst, James Frederic, and associates. *America's Needs and Re-sources: A New Survey.* New York: Twentieth Century Fund, 1955.

Diebold, William, Jr. *The United States and the Industrial World: American Foreign Economic Policy in the 1970s.* New York: Praeger, 1972.

Dowd, Douglas F., ed. *America's Role in the World Economy: The Challenge to Orthodoxy,* with reprinted publications by G. Haberler, J. K. Galbraith, James Tobin, Jan Tinbergen and Gunnar Myrdal. Studies in Economics. Boston: D.C. Heath, 1966.

Easterlin, Richard A., *Population, Labor Force, and Long Swings in Economic Growth: The American Experience,* National Bu-reau of Economic Research, no. 86, New York, 1968.

Friedman, Milton, and Schwartz, Anna Jacobson. *A Monetary His-tory of the United States, 1867–1960,* National Bureau of Economic Research, Studies in Business Cycles, no. 12. Princeton, N.J.: Princeton University Press, 1963.

Galbraith, John Kenneth. *The New Industrial State.* Boston: Hough-ton-Mifflin, 1967.

Goldsmith, Raymond William. *A Study of Saving in the United States.* 3 vols. Princeton, N.J.: Princeton University Press, 1955.

———. *Financial Intermediaries in the American Economy since 1900.* Princeton, N.J.: Princeton University Press, 1958.

———. *The National Wealth of the United States in the Postwar Period.* Princeton, N.J.: Princeton University Press, 1962.

Gordon, Robert A. *Business Fluctuations.* 2nd ed. New York: Harper and Brothers, 1961.

Harris, Seymour E. *Economics of the Kennedy Years—And a Look Ahead.* New York: Harper and Row, 1964.

Harris, Seymour E., ed. *The Dollar in Crisis*. New York: Harcourt, Brace and World, 1961.

Heller, Walter W. *New Dimensions of Political Economy*. Cambridge, Mass.: Harvard University Press, 1966.

Higgs, Robert. *The Transformation of the American Economy 1865–1914: An Essay in Interpretation*. The Wiley Series in American Economic History. New York: John Wiley and Sons, 1971.

Hoffmeyer, Erik. *Dollar Shortage and the Structure of U.S. Foreign Trade*. Copenhagen: Ejnar Manskgaard; Amsterdam: North Holland Publishing Co., 1958.

Katona, George. *The Powerful Consumer*. New York: McGraw-Hill, 1960.

Kendrick, John W., assisted by Maude R. Pech. *Productivity Trends in the United States*. A Study by the National Bureau of Economic Research, New York. Princeton, N.J.: Princeton University Press, 1961.

Kershaw, Joseph A., assisted by Paul N. Courant. *Government against Poverty*. Studies in Social Economics. Washington, D.C.: The Brookings Institution, 1970.

Kuznets, Simon Smith, assisted by Elizabeth Jenks. "Capital in the American Economy: Its Formation and Financing," a study by the National Bureau of Economic Research, Princeton, N.J.: Princeton University Press, 1961.

―――. "National Income, 1919–1938," National Bureau of Economic Research, Occasional paper 2, New York, April, 1941.

―――, assisted by Lillian Epstein and Elizabeth Jenks. *National Income and Its Composition, 1919–1938*. New York: National Bureau of Economic Research, 1941.

―――, assisted by Lillian Epstein and Elizabeth Jenks. *National Product since 1869*. New York: National Bureau of Economic Research, 1946.

―――. *Population Redistribution and Economic Growth: United States, 1870–1950*. 3 vols. Under direction of Simon Kuznets and Dorothy Swaine Thomas. Philadelphia: The American Philosophical Society, 1957–1964.

―――. *Shares of Upper Income Groups in Income and Savings*. Occasional paper no. 35. New York: National Bureau of Economic Research, 1950.

Landsberg, Hans H.; Fischman, Leonard L.; and Fisher, Joseph L. *Resources in America's Future: Patterns of Requirements and Availabilities 1960–2000*. Baltimore: Johns Hopkins Press for Resources for the Future, Inc., 1963.

Leontief, Wassily. *Input-Output Economics*. New York: Oxford University Press, 1966.

Lindbeck, Assar. *The Political Economy of the New Left: An Outsider's View*. Foreword by Paul Samuelson. New York: Harper and Row, 1971.

Morgan, James N.; David, Martin H.; Cohen, Wilbur J.; and Brazer, Harvey E. *Income and Welfare in the United States.* New York: McGraw-Hill, 1962.

Moroney, J. R. *The Structure of Production in American Manufacturing.* Chapel Hill, N.C.: University of North Carolina Press, 1972.

Musgrave, Richard A., and Musgrave, Peggy B. *Public Finance in Theory and Practice.* New York: McGraw-Hill, 1973.

National Bureau of Economic Research. "Trends in the American Economy in the Nineteenth Century," Studies in Income and Wealth, vol. 24, by the Conference on Research in Income and Wealth. Princeton, N.J.: Princeton University Press, 1960.

North, Douglass C. *The Economic Growth of the United States, 1790–1860.* Englewood Cliffs, N.J.: Prentice-Hall, 1961.

Perloff, Harvey S.; Dunn, Jr., Edgar S.; Lampard, Eric E.; and Muth, Richard F. *Regions, Resources, and Economic Growth.* Baltimore: Johns Hopkins Press, 1960.

Reuss, Henry S. *The Critical Decade—An Economic Policy for America and the Free World.* New York: McGraw-Hill, 1964.

Schultz, George P., and Aliber, Robert Z., eds. *Guidelines, Informal Controls and the Market Place.* Chicago: University of Chicago Press, 1966.

Schultz, Theodore W. *Investment in Human Capital: The Role of Education and of Research.* New York: The Free Press; London: Collier-Macmillan, 1971.

Smith, Warren L., and Teigen, Ronald L., eds. *Readings in Money, National Income and Stabilization Policy.* Homewood, Ill.: Richard D. Irwin, 1965.

Stiglitz, Joseph E., ed. *The Collected Scientific Papers of Paul A. Samuelson.* 2 vols. Cambridge, Mass.: M.I.T. Press, 1966.

Tobin, James. *National Economic Policy.* New Haven, Conn.: Yale University Press, 1966.

Triffin, Robert. *Gold and the Dollar Crisis.* rev. ed. New Haven, Conn.: Yale University Press, 1961.

Vatter, Harold G. *The U.S. Economy in the 1950's—An Economic History.* New York: W. W. Norton, 1963.

White, L. J. *The Automobile Industry since 1945.* Cambridge, Mass.: Harvard University Press, 1971.

Williamson, Harold Francis, ed. *The Growth of the American Economy: An Introduction to the Economic History of the United States.* New York: Prentice-Hall, 1944.

Index

175

Karl W. Roskamp was born in Germany. Educated at the University of Göttingen, the Free University of Berlin, the University of Frankfurt, the University of Michigan, and Massachusetts Institute of Technology, he is a professor of economics at Wayne State University.

The book was edited by Saundra Blais. The book was designed by Judy Mussel. The typeface for the text is Caledonia based on an original design by W. A. Dwiggins about 1938; and the display face is Americana designed by Richard Isbell about 1967.

The text is printed on Bookmark paper and the book is bound in Columbia Mills' Triton cloth over binders boards. Manufactured in the United States of America.